Hedy's Folly

For Anthony and Denise

A grant from the Alfred P. Sloan Foundation supported the research for this book.

Contents

Hedy's Folly

THE LIFE AND BREAKTHROUGH INVENTIONS
OF HEDY LAMARR, THE MOST BEAUTIFUL
WOMAN IN THE WORLD

RICHARD RHODES

Doubleday New York London Toronto Sydney Auckland

www.doubleday.com

Grateful acknowledgment is made to the following for permission to reprint previously
published and unpublished material:

The Estate of George Antheil: Excerpts from *Bad Boy of Music* by George Antheil
(Doubleday, Doran & Company, Inc., 1945) and excerpts from the unpublished
writings and correspondence of George and Boski Antheil (Library of Congress
Antheil Collection). Reprinted by permission of The Estate of George Antheil,
administered by Charles Amirkhanian.

Viking Penguin, a division of Penguin Group (USA) Inc., and Williams Verlag AG:
Excerpts from *The World of Yesterday* by Stefan Zweig, translated by Helmut Ripperger
and Ben Huebsch, copyright © 1943 by the Viking Press, Inc. Rights to the underlying
work, copyright © 1977 by William Verlag AG, Zurich. Reprinted by permission of
Viking Penguin, a division of Penguin Group (USA) Inc., and Williams Verlag AG.

Jacket design by Michael J. Windsor
Jacket photo of Hedy Lamarr: Getty Images #2637880 © Hulton Archive/Getty Images

LIBRARY OF CONGRESS CATALOGING-IN-PUBLICATION DATA
Rhodes, Richard, 1937–
Hedy's folly : the life and breakthrough inventions of Hedy Lamarr, the most beautiful
woman in the world / Richard Rhodes.—1st ed.
p. cm.
Includes bibliographical references and index.
1. Lamarr, Hedy, 1913–2000. 2. Actresses—United States—Biography. 3. Motion
picture actors and actresses —United States—Biography.
4. Spread spectrum communications. I. Title.
PN2287.L24R54 2011
791.430'28092—dc23
[B]   2011021746

ISBN 978-0-385-53438-3
eBook ISBN 978-0-385-53439-0

MANUFACTURED IN THE UNITED STATES OF AMERICA

10 9 8 7 6

First Edition

Hedy Lamarr, Inventor

Invention is a strange business. Is it creative, like painting or sculpture? It's certainly original, by definition genuinely new, but it's also and fundamentally practical. Patent law says an idea must be "reduced to practice" to be patentable. That means an idea must be embodied in some new and useful mechanism or process or material. So invention is creative, but not in the same way the fine arts are. Usefulness isn't fundamental to a sculpture or a painting.

Is invention, then, scientific? Many inventions today are explicitly derived from scientific discoveries. The discovery that certain materials, stimulated in a particular way, would emit coherent light—light all of the same wavelength—led to the invention of the laser. The laser was a practical device that embodied the discovery, but it wasn't the discovery itself. The distinction is clear even in prescientific times: Fire was a discovery; the fireplace was an invention. That fire hardened clay was a discovery; pottery was an invention. Again, as with fine art, usefulness isn't a requirement for scientific discovery.

That invention is different from fine art or scientific discovery suggests that inventors might be different from artists or scientists. They are. Many inventors are technically trained, of course, especially those who invent professionally. Thomas Edison was home- and self-educated, but Nikola Tesla, the inventor of radio, was an electrical engineer. Some inventors have been artists. Samuel F. B. Morse, the co-inventor of the telegraph, was a professional painter. The same person might do science and invent. I knew such a person, a Nobel laureate American physicist named Luis Alvarez. Luis's many inventions won him a place in the National Inventors Hall of Fame. He told me once that he valued his recognition as an inventor more than the Nobel.

But many inventors, past and present, have been people with no obvious special qualifications for inventing. Come to think of it, there are no special qualifications for inventing. No school I know of offers such a degree. As a sculptor is someone who sculpts, as a writer is someone who writes, an inventor is someone who invents.

The 1940s Austrian-American movie star Hedy Lamarr was an inventor. The public-relations department at Metro-Goldwyn-Mayer, where Hedy began her American film career, put out the claim that she was "the most beautiful woman in the world," and by Western standards she may have been. It annoyed her deeply, however, that few people saw beyond her beauty to her intelligence. "Any girl can be glamorous," she famously and acidly said. "All you have to do is stand still and look stupid."

Hedy invented as a hobby. Since she made two or three movies a year, each one taking about a month to shoot, she had spare time to fill. She didn't drink and she didn't like to party, so she took up inventing. When she was a girl, her father, a Viennese banker, had encouraged her interest in how the world worked, taking walks with her and explaining the mechanics of the machinery they encountered. As a young woman, before she emigrated from Austria to the United States, she married a munitions manufacturer and listened in on the technical discussions he held with his Austrian and German military clients. She also had a keen sense of the world's large and small failings, some of which she decided she could fix. In Hollywood she set up an inventor's corner in the drawing room of her house, complete with a drafting table and lamp and all the necessary drafting tools.

Hedy conceived of her most important invention in 1941, in the dark years between the German invasion of Poland in September 1939 and the Japanese attack on Pearl Harbor in December 1941 that finally impelled the United States to enter the war. She wanted to help her newly adopted country (where she was still technically an enemy alien) and saw the need for a weapon to attack the German submarines that were devastating North Atlantic shipping. It's characteristic of her confidence in her inventive gift that she believed she could devise such a weapon and help change the course of the war. Her belief was folly in two senses of that fine old word: extravagant in consequential invention, and founded on the foolish notion that the United States Navy would take correction from a Hollywood actress of great beauty in a matter about which it was not prepared to listen to its own submarine commanders.

Her unlikely, but ideal, partner in that work was an avant-garde composer and concert pianist named George Antheil, at five feet four a "cello-sized man," as *Time* magazine put it, a New Jersey native whose father owned a shoe store. Antheil was not, like Hedy, an amateur inventor, but he was nearly polymathic in his gifts. When Hedy revealed her idea to him, he immediately saw a way to give it practical form for the purpose of patenting it.

That practical form linked back to Antheil's most notorious composition, a twenty-minute rhythmic cacophony of grand pianos, electric bells, drums, xylophones, a siren, a gong, an airplane propeller, and sixteen synchronized player pianos called *Ballet mécanique*, which premiered in Paris in 1926. In his Paris days, before he moved to Hollywood to make a living writing film scores, Antheil was a good friend of Ernest Hemingway, Igor Stravinsky, the bookseller Sylvia Beach (the Antheils lived for ten years in a small apartment on the mezzanine of Beach's famous Shakespeare and

Company bookstore), James Joyce, Ezra Pound, and most of the rest of the fabled crowd of expatriates who helped make Paris a world center of art, music, and literature in the years between the two world wars.

Hedy in Vienna, George in Paris, and then the two of them meeting up in Hollywood to invent a fundamental new wireless technology makes a remarkable story at the center of Hedy Lamarr's long and fascinating life. Except in the matter of her beauty, which she valued least of all, people regularly underestimated her. She deserved better. The real story will amaze you.

ONE

A Charming Austrian Girl

She was Viennese, not yet seventeen in the spring of 1931 but already a professional actress, in rehearsal for a play. Hedwig Kiesler (pronounced *HAYD-vig KEES-lur*)—Hedy—had won a small role in the Berlin incarnation of *The Weaker Sex*, which the celebrated Austrian impresario Max Reinhardt was directing. When Reinhardt restaged the play in Vienna that spring, she had single-mindedly quit the Berlin cast and followed him home. "Are you here too, Fraulein Kiesler?" he'd asked her in surprise. "Are you living with your family? All right, you can be the Americaness again." Édouard Bourdet's play was a comedy with a pair of boorish stage Americans as foils. Reinhardt had assigned the actor George Weller, Hedy's husband in the play, to teach her some American songs. "I took this as a mandate to make an American out of Hedy Kiesler," the young Bostonian recalled.

She was eager to be transformed. "Hedy had only the vaguest ideas of what the United States were," Weller discovered, "except that they were grouped around Hollywood." She idolized the California tennis star Helen Wills, "Little Miss Poker Face." Wills, focused and unexpressive on the courts, all business, was the world's number-one-ranked female tennis player, midway that year through an unbroken run of 180 victories. "Watch me look like Helen Wills," Hedy teased Weller when they rehearsed together. *"Du, schau' mal, hier bin ich Kleine Poker Face."* Her lively young face would grow calm, Weller remembered, "expressionless and assured, her brow would clarify, and for a moment she would really become an American woman." Commandeering the property room, Hedy and George practiced singing "Yes, Sir, That's My Baby," "Yes, We Have No Bananas," and an Austrian favorite, Al Jolson's lugubrious "Sonny Boy." It melted the matrons at matinees, many of them mothers with sons lost in the long slaughter of the Great War.

An only child, entertaining herself with her dolls, Hedy had dreamed since she was a little girl of becoming a movie star. "I had a little stage under my father's desk," she recalled, "where I would act out fairy tales. When someone would come into the room they would think my mind was really wandering. I was always talking to myself." Her tall, handsome, vigorous father, Emil, an athlete as well as a successful banker, told her stories, read her books, and took her on walks in their tree-lined neighborhood and in the great park of the Wienerwald—the Vienna Woods. Wherever they went together, he explained to her how everything worked— "from printing presses to streetcars," she said. Her father's enthusiasm for technology links her lifelong interest in invention with cherished memories of her favorite parent.

Hedy's mother was stricter, concerned that such a pretty, vivacious child would grow up spoiled unless she heard criticism as well as compliments. "She has always had everything," Trude Kiesler said. "She never had to long for anything. First there was her father who, of course, adored her, and was very proud of her. He gave her all the comforts, pretty clothes, a fine home, parties, schools, sports. He looked always for the sports for her, and music." Trude had trained as a concert pianist before motherhood intervened. In turn, she supervised Hedy's lessons on the grand piano in the Kiesler salon. "I underemphasized praise and flattery," Trude determined, "hoping in this way to balance the scales for her."

The Kieslers were assimilated Jews, Trude from Budapest, Emil from Lemberg (now known as Lviv). Hedy kept her Jewish heritage secret throughout her life; her son and daughter only learned of it after her death. In prewar Vienna it had hardly mattered. The Viennese population's mixed legacy of Slavic, Germanic, Hungarian, Italian, and Jewish traditions was one of its glories, one reason for the city's unique creative ferment in the first decades of the new century. Sigmund Freud's daughters attended the same girls' middle school that Hedy later did, and after the war Anna Freud taught there.

Vienna is an old city, with ruins dating to Roman times.

The emperor Marcus Aurelius wrote his third book of *Meditations* on that rough Germanic frontier. Set in the broad Danube valley at the eastern terminus of the Alps, it grew across the centuries through great turmoil to become the capital of the Austro-Hungarian Empire. A wide ring boulevard supplanted its medieval wall after 1857, opening it up to its suburbs. By 1910, two million ethnically diverse Viennese, reading newspapers published in ten languages, took their leisure in sparkling coffeehouses, and the beneficence of the emperor Franz Josef had filled the city's twenty-one districts with parks, statues, and palaces. To the Viennese writer Stefan Zweig, his birthplace was "a city of a thousand attractions, a city with theatres, museums, bookstores, universities, music, a city in which each day brought new surprises."

If Vienna was old, it made itself radically modern in the years around the Great War in music, theater, and art. Austrian culture had prepared the way, Zweig believed: "Precisely because the monarchy, because Austria itself for centuries had been neither politically ambitious nor particularly successful in military actions, the native pride had turned more strongly toward a desire for artistic supremacy." Vienna was the arena of that desire. The roll call of important early-twentieth-century artists, musicians, writers, scientists, and philosophers active in the Viennese milieu is startling: the artists Gustav Klimt, Josef Hoffmann, Egon Schiele, and Oskar Kokoschka; the writers Hugo von Hofmannsthal, Arthur Schnitzler, Robert Musil, and Joseph Roth; the composers Gustav Mahler, Arnold Schoenberg, Anton von Webern, and Alban Berg. Sigmund Freud invented psychoanalysis in Vienna. Ludwig Boltzmann and Ernst Mach contributed importantly to physics there. Rudolf Carnap, Kurt Gödel, Otto Neurath, and, most famously, Ludwig Wittgenstein transformed philosophy.

"The whole city was at one," Zweig saw, in its "receptivity for all that was colorful, festive and resounding, in [its] pleasure in the theatrical, whether it was on the stage or in reality, both as theatre and as a mirror of life." For Zweig, theater was the core Viennese experience:

> It was not the military, nor the political, nor the commercial, that was predominant in the life of the individual and of the masses. The first glance of the average Viennese into his morning paper was not at the events in parliament, or world affairs, but at the repertoire of the theatre, which assumed so important a role in public life as hardly was possible in any other city. For the Imperial theatre, the Burgtheater, was for the Viennese and for the Austrian more than a stage upon which actors enacted parts; it was the microcosm that mirrored the macrocosm, the brightly colored reflection in which the city saw itself. . . . The stage, instead of being merely a place of entertainment, was a spoken and plastic guide of good behavior and correct pronunciation, and a nimbus of respect encircled like a halo

everything that had even the faintest connection with the Imperial theatre.

What else but theater, and by extension motion pictures, would a bright, pretty, single-minded Viennese girl choose? "I acted all the time," Hedy recalled. "I copied my mother. I copied the way she walked and the way she talked. I copied her mannerisms, her facial expression. I copied the guests who came to our house. I copied people I saw in the streets. I copied the servants. I was a little living copybook. I wrote people down on me."

Acting was in the air. In his school classes, Zweig remembered, "in keeping with the Viennese atmosphere . . . the impulse to creative production became positively epidemic. Each of us sought some talent within himself and endeavored to unfold it." Four or five of Zweig's classmates wanted to be actors. "They imitated the diction of the Imperial players, they recited and declaimed without ceasing, secretly took lessons in acting, and, during the recesses at school, distributed parts and improvised entire scenes from the classics, while the rest of us formed a curious but exacting audience."

Hedy took more direct action, as her father had taught her. "He made me understand that I must make my own decisions," she said, "mold my own character, think my own thoughts." She had met Max Reinhardt, the director and impresario, at a party in 1929, when she was fifteen, and he had seemed interested in her. "He had encouraged me by telling me to hold fast to my dream and that if I held fast it would come true." She held fast, and it did.

After an unhappy term at a Swiss finishing school that she finessed by running away home to Vienna, she scouted a motion-picture studio, Sascha-Film, the largest in the city. To buy time for her assault, she added a zero to a school absence request her mother had signed, turning one hour into ten—two school days. "I knew that the studio employed script girls. I did not have any idea of what script girls are supposed to do, but I knew that they were on the sets all the time watching the actors work—and that was enough for me." She slipped into the studio and presented herself. "They asked me, 'Do you know how to be a script girl?' and I said, 'No. But may I try?'" Probably because she was pretty as well as brash, the script supervisor laughed and took her on.

She had that day and one more to make good. The film then in production was called *Geld auf der Strasse* (*Money in the Streets*). There was a minor part for a girl in a nightclub scene. "I applied for it and right away I got it," Hedy recalled. In this account, for an American magazine, she translates her starting salary as "five dollars a day."

Then she had to tell her parents that she was dropping out of school at sixteen to become a professional actress. As she remembered the negotiation in 1938:

> Well, it was not too bad. They were bewildered a little but not very surprised. They were never *surprised* at

anything I did. And besides, I had been talking movies for so long that they were really prepared for this. My dear father finally laughed and said, "You have been an actress ever since you were a baby!" So my parents did not try to prevent me. They were willing to give me this great wish of my heart.

She recalled it differently later in life. She had persuaded the director, Georg Jacoby, to give her the part. Her parents, she wrote, "were much more difficult to persuade than [Jacoby], because it meant my dropping school. But at last they agreed. My father had never forbidden his little princess anything, and besides, he reasoned that I would soon enough quit of my own accord and go back to school."

When *Geld auf der Strasse* wrapped, a better role followed as a secretary in *Sturm im Wasserglas* (*Storm in a Water Glass*), another Jacoby project. Then Reinhardt cast her in *The Weaker Sex*. "Reinhardt made me read, meet people, attend plays." She followed him back to Vienna when he restaged the play there. "Yes, we have no bananas."

"When you dance with her," George Weller remembered, "as I did every night for about three months, she is a trifle stiff to the touch. Reedlike, that's what Hedy Kiesler is, sweet and reedlike, and when she wants to talk to you she doesn't lean over your shoulder and arch herself out behind like a debutante. . . . She leans back from you [and] takes a good look in your eyes and a firm grip on your name before she will allow herself to say a word."

Weller was present when Reinhardt gave Hedy her life-long byname, a christening later claimed by the Hollywood studio head Louis B. Mayer:

It was at the rehearsal of a cafe scene in a comedy, and the *Regisseur* [that is, the director] was Reinhardt. There were Viennese newspapermen watching. Suddenly the Herr Professor, a man not given to superlatives, turned to the reporters and mildly pronounced these words: "Hedy Kiesler is the most beautiful girl in the world." Instantly the reporters put it down. In five minutes the Herr Professor's sentence, utter and absolute, had been telephoned to the newspapers of the [city center], to be dispatched by press services to other newspapers, other capitals, countries, continents.

The Weaker Sex played in Vienna for one month, from 8 May to 8 June 1931. "Almost before we knew it," Weller recalled, "another play was in rehearsal." Hollywood was buying up European actors as it rapidly expanded film production, a trend that would accelerate after 1933 when the Nazis took power in Germany and then in Austria, and Jews saw their civil rights stripped away. The play, *Film und Liebe (Film and Love)*, satirized the earlier, commercial phase of the exodus. Weller won the role of "a brash Hollywood director who thought . . . that Central European talent could be seduced by American gold into immigrating to California."

The female lead as Weller remembered it called for a character "who simply recoiled at the sight of a Hollywood contract," which would have been a stretch for Hedy. In any case the director offered her a smaller role.

She rejected it. "I've never been satisfied," she explained. "I've no sooner done one thing than I am seething inside me to do another thing. And so, almost as soon as I was inside a studio I wanted to be acting in a studio. And as soon as I was acting in a studio, I wanted to be starring in a studio. I wanted to be famous." Her stage roles had been limited and her reviews mixed. Weller thought she simply "decided for herself . . . that she wanted no more stage."

Berlin was the center of filmmaking, and to Berlin she returned that August 1931, looking for work. She found it with the Russian émigré director Alexis Granowsky, who cast her as the mayor's daughter in a comedy, *Die Koffer des Herrn O.F.* (*The Trunks of Mr. O.F.*). The cast included her rising Austrian contemporary Peter Lorre in his fourth film role. When *Trunks* wrapped, in mid-October, Sascha-Film obligingly offered her the female lead in another comedy to be shot in Berlin, *Man braucht kein Geld* (*One Needs No Money*), opposite Heinz Rühmann, a German film star. Hedy turned seventeen midway through the November production. *Die Koffer des Herrn O.F.* premiered in Berlin on 2 December. *Man braucht kein Geld* followed in Vienna on 22 December. "Excellent work by a cast of familiar German actors," the *New York Times* would praise *Man braucht kein Geld* on its

New York opening the following fall, "reinforced by Hedy Kiesler, a charming Austrian girl." It was her first American notice.

Then a truly starring role came to hand. The Czech director Gustav Machatý found Hedy in Berlin and offered her the lead in a Czechoslovakian film, *Ekstase* (*Ecstasy*), a love story. She was thrilled. "When I had this opportunity to star in [the film]," she recalled, "it was the biggest opportunity I had had. I was mad for this chance, of course." Shooting was scheduled for July 1932. To fill the intervening months, she replaced one of the four actors in Noël Coward's comedy *Private Lives* at the Komödie Theatre.

Whether or not Hedy's parents read the script of *Ekstase* isn't clear from the remaining record. Since she was still a minor, however, they did try to protect her:

> I could not go, my father said, unless my mother went too. But I did not want my mother to go. . . . I was young enough to want to be on my own. What kind of a baby, what kind of an amateur would they think me, I said, if I had to have my mother along to take care of me! Besides, I felt embarrassed when my mother was in the studio, was on the sets watching me. I felt stiff and self-conscious then. I could not feel free and grownup like that. I finally prevailed upon my father to allow me to go with the members of the company. There could be no harm in this.

Eventually, she revealed another reason she had insisted on traveling unaccompanied: "I went to Prague because I was in love with somebody." She wanted no chaperoning mother to interfere.

Hedy's performance as Eva in *Ekstase* would both promote and plague her professional career. Although the film includes a brief nude scene, it's guileless rather than salacious. A young wife, Eva, languishes in an unconsummated marriage to a fussy middle-aged man. Frustrated, she leaves him. Out riding one morning, enjoying her new freedom, she stops to swim in a woodland pond, parking her summer playsuit on the back of her unsaddled mare. While she's swimming, her mare runs away, attracted to a stallion in the next pasture. Adam, a handsome engineer on a road construction crew, stripped to the waist and a-sweat, catches the runaway and goes looking for its rider. He finds Eva hiding behind a bush and tosses her playsuit to her. Dressed, disdainfully retrieving her horse, she trips and sprains her ankle. He splints it, necessarily handling her leg, and she slaps him for his familiarity. Back home, she realizes she's drawn to him, struggles with her feelings, finally looks him up in his construction cabin and initiates a night of passion. Afterward the lovers happily plan another night together at a hotel.

The next day they go into town separately to avoid scandal. Adam catches a ride unknowingly with Eva's husband, Emile, who recognizes as his estranged wife's a necklace Adam is fondling. Both men check into the same hotel. The engineer hires musicians to serenade Eva as they drink champagne and dance on the hotel terrace. Emile in his room overhead hears the music and agonizes. There's a shot. The hotel staff crowds around the door to Emile's room. Adam breaks in: Emile has killed himself, his fussy pince-nez lying broken on the floor. Adam and Eva go to the station to wait for the next train to Berlin. He falls asleep. She decides to return home and leaves him sleeping—their night of passion was a deliverance but not an obligation.

In this simple and largely pantomimed story, only three brief scenes challenge what would otherwise be at most a PG-13 rating today: a glimpse of Eva's breasts as she swims nude, a long shot of her running nude through the woods, and a gauzy close-up of her face in passion during the couple's night of lovemaking. Not nudity but blatant Freudian symbolism communicates the film's sexual themes: a jackhammer drilling, a bee pollinating a flower, a stallion rearing and snorting before servicing a mare off camera. More challenging than nudity or symbolism to the sexual canons of the day, in America in particular, was the story itself, which reversed the prevailing Victorian paternalism. Eva falls for Adam, seeks him out, seduces him, takes her pleasure, and drops him when she's done, while Emile, when he realizes he isn't vital enough for her, obligingly shoots himself. Had the film been released in the 1960s instead of the 1930s, it might have been hailed as feminist.

Certainly *Ekstase* embodied the new spirit of personal

freedom which Zweig observed of that time and place. "The world began to take itself more youthfully," he writes, "and, in contrast to the world of my parents, was proud of being young. . . . To be young and fresh, and to get rid of pompous dignity, was the watchword of the day. The women threw off the corsets which had confined their breasts, and abjured parasols and veils since they no longer feared air and sunshine. They shortened their skirts so that they could use their legs freely at tennis, and were no longer bashful about displaying them if they were pretty ones. Fashions became more natural; men wore breeches, women dared to ride astride, and people no longer covered up and hid themselves from one another."

Ekstase illustrates these changes both in situation and in costume. It also dramatizes the corresponding changes in values that Zweig observed:

> This health and self-confidence of the generation that succeeded mine won for itself freedom in modes and manners as well. For the first time girls were seen without governesses on excursions with their young friends, or participating in sports in frank, self-assured comradeship; they were no longer timid or prudish, they knew what they wanted and what they did not want. Freed from the anxious control of their parents, earning their own livelihood as secretaries or office workers, they seized the right to live their own

lives. Prostitution, the only love institution which the old world sanctioned, declined markedly, for because of this newer and healthier freedom all manner of false modesty had become old-fashioned. In the swimming-places the wooden fences which had inexorably separated the women's section from the men's were torn down, and men and women were no longer ashamed to show how they were built. More freedom, more frankness, more spontaneity had been regained in these ten years [after the turn of the century] than in the previous hundred years.

As if confirming Zweig's insight, Hedy announced during the production of *Ekstase* that she had been offered a Hollywood contract and had turned it down. "I don't want to become the slave of film," she told an Austrian magazine grandly, "but rather want to make films or take breaks when I feel like it."

After filming *Ekstase*, she returned to Vienna. In November she celebrated her eighteenth birthday. She was ill with influenza and lost weight, enhancing her already striking beauty. When she recovered, she nearly won the role of Caroline Esterhazy, the young Hungarian countess whom Franz Schubert tutored and loved, in the film *Unfinished Symphony*. She was reluctantly passed over because the role required someone who could sing Schubert art songs and she was not a trained singer.

Ekstase premiered in Prague on 20 January 1933. At

that distance it was relatively painless. A month later, its Vienna premiere simultaneously in four theaters drew large crowds—more than seventy thousand tickets sold in its first two weeks. Hedy prepared her parents for the experience by warning them that the film was "artistic," but nothing prepared them for seeing their daughter nude or apparently having sex. "I wanted to run and hide," she remembered. "My father solved the predicament. He simply rose and said grimly, 'We will go.' I gathered my belongings in one grab. My mother seemed angry, but somehow reluctant to walk out. Nevertheless, walk out we did."

"My mother and father suffered about it," Hedy acknowledged. "My father suffered even more than my mother, I think. It was the hurt look in his eyes that made me realize to the full how silly and ill-advised I had been." They were told, she said, that they should "do something" about it, "that I was a minor and that the company had no right to ask such a thing of me. . . . But my father felt, and rightly, that to make a fuss about it would only attract more publicity to it." She made him understand, she said, how when you're young you're "apt to do foolish things in an effort to appear experienced and of the world. And so, because they loved me very dearly, they did not speak of it any more."

Publicity scandals that feel like the end of the world usually aren't. Fritz Kreisler, the violinist and composer, had written a musical comedy about what *Time* magazine would describe as "the courtship of the young Emperor Franz Josef and

Elizabeth, 16-year-old, harum-scarum daughter of Bavaria's Duke Max." Elizabeth's nickname was Sissy; she was, *Time* explained, "the favorite of her father who roved the forests with woodcutter friends, played the zither, behaved more like a peasant than a duke." *Sissy* had opened in Vienna's Theater an der Wien just at Christmas 1932; it would continue through hundreds of performances. Musical comedy didn't require the classically trained singing voice that Schubert lieder did. Hedy understudied the role of Sissy beginning in early January 1933 and took over the lead in late March. "At first I felt reluctant about it," she remembered. "I said to myself, 'How will they accept me as the Austrian Queen after this 'Ecstasy'? But the [theater] prevailed upon me and of course I really wanted to." The audience welcomed her, as did a reviewer: "She looks wonderful, tender and really attractive. And she performs with real charm too: simply without affectation, talking and singing with the high voice of a child. . . . In short, a delightful Sissy, without the stardom and pomp of a sophisticate, but with easy, childlike tones."

Flowers began to crowd Hedy's dressing room that spring, tokens from a wealthy admirer. She wasn't impressed. "From the first night Fritz Mandl saw me on the stage," she recalled, "he tried, in every way, to get in touch with me. He sent me flowers, quantities of flowers. I sent them back to him." Though she had never met him, Mandl was not unknown to her. "I had heard of him, of course, as who in Austria had not? I knew of his high position, his wealth, his connection with the foreign powers. The flowers he sent me seemed like a 'command performance.' I did not like that."

Friedrich "Fritz" Mandl was a heavyweight, thirty-three years old and the third-richest man in Austria. His wealth had originated in a family-owned ammunition factory in Hirtenberg, a small town about twenty-five miles southwest of Vienna, which had begun making rifle cartridges for the armies of Europe soon after their invention in America during the Civil War. Mandl's father, Alexander, had hired him to rebuild the Hirtenberger Patronen-Fabrik in the aftermath of its nearly complete destruction by arson during labor troubles in 1920, and in 1924 he became general manager. By the time Mandl began courting Hedy, a historian writes, "he had negotiated agreements with arms manufacturers in France, Germany, and Italy, and controlled arms plants in Poland, Switzerland, Austria, and the Netherlands."

Having failed to win Hedy's attention with notes and flowers, Mandl called her mother at home. "He introduced himself," Hedy said, "and then he asked my mother if he might come to our house to meet me. My mother did not know how to say 'no' to what was, after all, a legitimate request." Trude Kiesler mentioned a day, and Mandl turned up hat in hand.

He was not a tall man; in photographs he appears to be no taller than Hedy, who was five feet seven. His head was large, his face fleshy, his body stocky and apparently powerful. *Time* would describe him at this point in his life as "a young viveur who gambled for high stakes, and kept fancy apartments." He was half-Jewish; his Jewish father, Alexander, had fallen in love with a family chambermaid who was Catholic and had converted to her faith and married her after Fritz was born. By all accounts Fritz was a womanizer and an arriviste, already once divorced. He was also a canny and ruthless businessman. "He was so powerful," Hedy said, "so influential, so rich, that always he had been able to arrange everything in his life just as he wished it. . . . The afternoon he first came I was, I am afraid, very rude to him. . . . It was the first clash of our wills. There were to be many."

If Mandl had not been smitten before, Hedy's disdain beguiled him. The courtship began:

He asked me to go to dinner with him that night. But I would not go. He then telephoned to me every day, many times a day, and asked me to dine, to dance, after the theatre. At first I would not go. He would come again and again to my house, which was the only place where I would receive him. And every night he would be in the theatre. And every night and in the daytimes he would send great baskets and boxes of flowers.

When he came to my house he talked to me about hunting, which he loves and which I also love. He told me about his munitions factory. He explained how his father had built the factory but how when he, Fritz, was nineteen years old, the factory burned to the ground and much of the fortune was wiped out and how he had

had to build it all up again, the factory and the fortune
too. So that he had really made the fortune himself.
This gave me a different idea of him from the one I had
had. This was not inherited power. This was the stuff of
power itself. I liked that.

Hedy's model of a man was her father, but if her father was
a frigate, Mandl was a battleship:

I began to feel attracted by the brain of the man, by
his tremendous power, by his charm which, when
he wished, could be as powerful as his brain. I love
strength. I *love* it. I think that all women love strength
in a man. . . .
    Then, suddenly, he was the most beautiful—no, I
mean the most attractive—man in the world to me.
    And I knew that I was in love with him, madly in
love with him.
    We became engaged as soon as I knew this and I was
terribly happy. I was in love. I was happy. I was proud.
I was proud of him. I was proud of myself. I was proud
of his brilliance and strength and power. . . .
    He had the most amazing brain. . . . There was
nothing he did not know. There was not a question I,
or anyone else, could ask him that he could not answer.
Ask him a formula in chemistry and he would give it
to you. Ask him about the habits of wild animals, how

glass is made, what about the laws of gravitation—
politics, of course, since he was so powerful a figure in
world politics and—well, "I don't know" was not in
him. He knew *everything*.

So, then, he seemed to have everything, Fritz Mandl.

So, then, he had Hedwig Kiesler as well.

Hedy left the cast of *Sissy* at the end of July 1933 to
prepare for her wedding. She remembered the 10 August
event as "small and quiet. . . . I wanted it to be quiet," she
explained. "He was so well known. And I, too, was known.
I did not want a carnival made of what belonged to him and
to me alone." But the setting for this small and quiet wedding
was Vienna's majestic eighteenth-century Baroque Karls-
kirche with its elongated dome and spiraled double columns,
its extensive frescoes and marble-and-gold-leafed sanctu-
ary flooded with light. Who was in attendance? Her mother
and father? Friends from the theater? She doesn't say. And
Mandl? Hedy was a trophy wife. Wouldn't he have wanted to
present her to Vienna?

However many attended the wedding, the newlyweds
went off afterward to the Lido, the fashionable barrier island
that divides the lagoon of Venice from the sea, to honey-
moon. "Almost at once," Hedy realized, "I found that I was
no longer Hedy Kiesler, an individual. But I was only the
wife of Fritz Mandl." Around this time Mandl is remembered
to have said: "Democracy is a luxury that might be borne,

perhaps, in prosperous periods." One of the first things her new husband did, Hedy said, was "try to track down and buy up every print of *Ekstase*. He spent a fortune trying to buy up that picture so that no print of it could ever be seen again. It was an obsession with him." *Time* would report Mandl spent "nearly $300,000" snapping up prints of the film, which of course multiplied like rabbits. Eventually, he gave up, but Hedy lamented that "it became one of the sore spots of our married life. Every time we would have an argument, no matter what about, he would, of course, bring that picture up to me. He would never let me forget it."

Nor would Mandl permit her to follow her career:

I knew very soon that I could never be an actress while I was his wife. When I was first married I did not think I would care. I thought, being so madly in love, that I could be content just as his wife. I soon found out that I could not be content anywhere but on the stage or screen. Perhaps if I had had children, perhaps if I had had something to *do*—but I was like a doll in a beautiful, jeweled case. I was watched and guarded and followed night and day. I could not go anywhere, not even to lunch with a woman friend, without being watched.

My husband bought a town house that was like a palace. Every piece in it was antique and priceless. We had also three hunting lodges. We had cars and planes and a yacht. We had many, many servants. I had furs

and jewels and gowns beyond any girl's wildest dreams
of luxury. . . .

[But] in my houses I had nothing to say. Not about
anything. . . . He ordered the house and everything in
it. . . . He was the absolute monarch in his own world.
He was the absolute monarch in his marriage. . . . I was
like a guest living in my own house. I was like a doll.
I was like a thing, some object of art which had to be
guarded—and imprisoned—having no mind, no life of
its own.

As Frau Hedwig Kiesler Mandl turned nineteen that
November 1933, she found herself locked into what she
would call a "prison of gold." Marriage to Fritz Mandl had
seemed to be another kind of stardom, a stardom of the real
world, radiant with power, but in its pursuit she had entered
unsuspectingly into a golden prison. The question now was,
how could she bear to live there? And if she couldn't, how on
earth could she get out?

TWO

Bad Boy of Music

A young American composer whose path would intersect
Hedy's in Hollywood was writing radical music in Paris while
she was still a girl. Born with the century in Trenton, New
Jersey, George Antheil (pronounced *ANT-hile*) had made
his way to Europe in 1922 as a concert pianist performing
both classical and modern works but emphasizing his own.
He was small, about five feet four; *Time* would describe him
colorfully as "a cello-sized man with blond hair and childlike
blue eyes." A nose flattened in a childhood accident made his
choirboy face pugilistic, however, and his tireless intensity
gave him scale. "He did nothing but write music and play
it on the piano," his playwright friend Ben Hecht recalled,
"which he made sound like a calliope in a circus parade." His
fellow composer Aaron Copland assessed Antheil's technique
more professionally: "When I first went to Paris I was jeal-

ous of Antheil's piano playing—it was so brilliant; he could demonstrate so well what he wanted to do."

What Antheil wanted to do was to create a distinctively American music, an ambition he conceived at seventeen while still living at home:

> Curiously enough, my springboard on this momen-
> tous occasion was not any American music I knew,
> nor American folksong, nor American composers of
> the past. It was, rather, a sudden acquaintanceship
> with the works of the Russian Five, that nationalist
> group of Russian composers chief amongst whom were
> Mussorgsky and Rimsky-Korsakov and, most of all
> composers, Tchaikovsky. Mussorgsky, particularly,
> charmed me, and I gathered at the Trenton, New
> Jersey, public library all the information about him
> and the Russian Five that was available.
>
> The information that I gathered enchanted me; I
> was, at the time, completely ripe for the musical phi-
> losophy of nationalism which the Russian Five had
> once preached and lived.

Antheil's early ambition matched the program for Ameri-can music championed by the New Yorker Paul Rosenfeld, the most influential music critic of the day. "I myself was present as a young man of 20," Antheil recalled, "when . . . Rosen-feld called a meeting of the four or five young American composers he then considered talented, in his apartment near Gramercy Place. . . . The upshot of that meeting was roughly something like this: 'The Russian Five could do it; why can't we?' It was, mainly, agreed that . . . we needed a housecleaning and a nationalist objective."

Antheil found inspiration for his new American music not in the United States but in Europe. "When I was 17," he wrote later, "in 1917, I used to go to sleep with a score of [Stravinsky's] 'Sacre du Printemps' and Schönberg's 'Fünf Orchestra Stücke' under my pillow." The problem was how to get to Europe when he was without money or immediate prospects. In 1921 he was forced to go hungry even to pay for composition lessons until his teacher found out and generously refunded his fees. When the refund depleted in turn, he went to see his mentor and former music teacher Constantin von Sternberg. "I told him I was broke and that I was getting rather tired of it," Antheil recalled with more bravado than he'd felt at the time. Sternberg sent him to the Philadelphia Main Line with a sealed letter to a wealthy American patron, Mary Louise Curtis Bok. Bok was the only child of Cyrus Curtis, whose Curtis Publishing owned both the *Ladies' Home Journal* and the *Saturday Evening Post*. The letter she read while Antheil waited in her parlor that afternoon described him as "one of the richest and strongest talents for composition that I have ever met here or in Europe." It asked her to give the young man "the means to hide himself for a year or two in some secluded spot . . . where . . . he could devote himself to his work without having to earn money for his bodily maintenance."

Bok responded to Sternberg's appeal, she told Antheil later, "on the basis of a young man possibly gifted for composition, actually a good pianist and very definitely an ill and starving boy." She set him up as a teacher at the Settlement Music School in Philadelphia, with a generous monthly stipend of $150—the equivalent of $1,700 today.

The following spring, well fed and comfortable but no less eager to work abroad, Antheil seized his chance. Learning that a young concert pianist had fallen out with the impresario M. H. Hanson, leaving a hole in Hanson's European concert commitments, Antheil set himself to practicing sixteen to twenty hours a day, soaking his hands in fishbowls of cold water when they swelled. "In this way," he wrote, "I gained a technique which, when a month later I played for Hanson, took him off his feet." Taking Hanson off his feet would have required great percussive force, which Antheil was already known for; the concert manager was "the exact duplicate of [the corpulent Hollywood actor] Sydney Greenstreet."

Hanson needed money to finance an Antheil concert tour. The ambitious young pianist turned again to Mary Louise Bok, as he would repeatedly for the next fifteen years, until her remarkable patience with his wheedling finally ran out. He told her why concertizing around Europe would be good for him, then sicced Hanson on her. Hanson described two tours, plain and deluxe, at $3,900 ($44,000 today) or $6,400

($72,000 today). Not wishing to seem ungenerous, Mrs. Bok chose the deluxe. Twenty-one-year-old George Antheil, child prodigy, high-school dropout, concert pianist, and incipient avant-garde composer, left for Europe in style. His *real* reason for going to Europe, he claimed long after, was to chase down a young woman he was in love with. Her mother had spirited her off to prevent their engagement, "to either Italy or Germany, probably the latter." But he also revealed that he had actually given up on her "the day she had disappeared without leaving me a clue." If he encountered her, it would only be to "silently reproach her," he fantasized, and then "sadly turn on my heel and walk away." At another time he explained that he went to Europe because, "first, I wanted to learn how to write better music; secondly, I wanted that music to be heard by publics more likely to be receptive to it than any I was likely to encounter in the America of 1922; and thirdly, the little money I had would last longer in Europe." None of these explanations is mutually exclusive. Europe—cheap, permissive, and reemergent—was a siren call for talented young Americans in the years after the Great War.

Antheil sailed with Hanson on the *Empress of Scotland* in May 1922. He performed in London to mixed reviews and detoured to southern Germany for an all-Teutonic music festival before setting up a base camp in Berlin. He spoke German like a native; his German-immigrant parents had spoken the language at home.

Hyperinflation was rapidly impoverishing the defeated citizens of Weimar Germany. The mark, which had stabilized at 320 to the U.S. dollar during the first half of 1922, would sink to 8,000 to the dollar by December, and that was only the beginning; by December 1923 the exchange rate would be 4.2 trillion marks to the dollar. That summer of 1922, Antheil remembered, "the girls and wives of some of the best families of Berlin were out on the street. Everything else had been hocked. Now they were hocking themselves, in order to eat." He was too young and too recently released from living at home not to take advantage of the opportunity. "There were just too many women. The men of Germany had mostly been killed off, or were crippled. In any case, the men left over were as poor and as starving as the women." So, inevitably, "it was curious to be a young foreigner with money, enough money, in Berlin in those days."

To his credit, Antheil shared his income from performing with fellow artists. "George was a tremendously generous person and somewhat childlike," his future wife would say of him, "and he helped a lot of artists at this time by buying paintings, inviting them to dinner, even supporting a few. It was all rather odd because he himself had no money, except what he made off the concerts, but there was some arrangement with his manager that he was paid in dollars, and dollars were at an incredible rate of exchange in the midst of the worst inflation."

Igor Stravinsky, one of Antheil's idols, turned up in Berlin that summer. He had been negotiating since the end of the Russian Revolution to reunite with his mother, still living in what was now the Soviet Union. The Soviet authorities had finally agreed to allow her to emigrate, and she was due to arrive on a Soviet ship at Stettin (now Szczecin, Poland), then a German port on the Baltic Sea, ninety miles northeast of Berlin. The Russian composer, who knew he had to meet his mother on the dock and personally shepherd her through German immigration or risk her deportation back to the U.S.S.R., had expected to wait in Berlin for no more than a week. Repeated delays in the ship's departure kept him waiting there for two months. When Antheil presented himself one morning at the Russischer Hof as an American composer and an admirer, Stravinsky welcomed him. They had breakfast together; Antheil showed Stravinsky the most Stravinsky-like of his compositions; Stravinsky asked him to lunch the next day. "Thereafter," Antheil perhaps exaggerates, "for two straight months, he and I had lunch together (and also, more often than not, breakfast, dinner, and supper), talking about everything in the contemporary world of music." In particular they talked "about mechanistic and percussive music," which was the kind Antheil was beginning to compose. When Stravinsky's mother finally arrived and the composer prepared to return with her to Paris, he offered to arrange a piano concert there for Antheil. "You play my music exactly as I wish it to be played," Antheil recalled him saying. "Really, I wish you would decide to come to Paris."

36

And so Antheil would, but not just yet. Settled that late autumn in a furnished apartment in the Berlin suburbs, waiting out the weeks until his midwinter concert tour would begin, he bought himself "an enormous fur coat made of Siberian cat," learned that the German fighter ace Rudolf Schultz-Dornburg, now the conductor of the Berlin Philharmonic, wanted to perform his First Symphony, and fell in love with the young Hungarian woman who would share his life, "a certain girl called Boski."

Boski (pronounced *BESH-key*) Markus was named after Elizabeth of Austria—Sissy, the same whom Hedy would play in Vienna in 1933. "I happened to be born in a little summer resort outside of Budapest," she recalled, "which was the summer residence of the Empress Elizabeth of Hungary-Austria . . . so my parents very imaginatively named me Elizabeth, which in Hungarian is *Erzsebet* or abbreviated: Boski." Antheil first saw her in a café near his apartment; she was simply dressed, "dark, had high cheekbones, but otherwise was delicately, rather sensitively beautiful." He asked around about her. A mutual acquaintance waved him off—she was "related to various well-to-do Viennese and Budapest families," the woman told him, but had "turned radical and run away from her family." She had been involved with the Communist revolution in Hungary after the war "and barely escaped Budapest with her life after its downfall." She was "only eighteen or nineteen, wild, untamable," a student at the University of Berlin. "She will hate you for an American capitalist," the woman concluded. A man who liked a challenge, Antheil was sold.

He invited Boski to the premiere of his First Symphony, assuming she'd be impressed, but she didn't like his music and left early. Undaunted, he arranged with their mutual friend to meet the two women for dinner two days before Christmas. He was due to leave on the midnight train to Paris, where Stravinsky had made good on his promise to set him up with a concert during Christmas week. When the mutual friend stepped out to make a phone call, Antheil sprang his plan on Boski: Christmas together in Paris. Nothing improper, he promised, just good fun. She confounded him by accepting the date but rejecting the location: the French were still denying visas to the citizens of their former Great War enemies, of which Hungary was one. Antheil was stuck. Either he played truant from performing for Stravinsky, or he revealed to Boski that their trip to Paris was an addendum to a concert commitment. "I was thunderstruck," he writes. "Boski Markus had said 'All right.' That was the main thing. Let Stravinsky wait."

Stravinsky did not take kindly to waiting. He substituted a French pianist, Jean Wiener, whom he praises in his autobiography without mentioning Antheil. But George and Boski began a lifelong relationship across a Christmas spent on the farm of an aunt of his in Poland.

It took the rest of the winter to work past Boski's resistance. "She represented much of that war-torn, disillusioned

Europe of 1923," Antheil writes; "I, a young, hopeful, but utterly naïve America of the same period." Boski recalled that "everybody was terribly poor at this time in Germany, and very, very bitter." The losses of the war, the punitive reparations that the victors had demanded, the worsening hyperinflation, all contributed to the German mood, which was turning violent. The Weimar Republic's foreign minister Walther Rathenau, though a nationalist himself, had been assassinated by two ultranationalist army officers the previous June. The small but burgeoning Nazi Party was mobilizing ever-larger rallies. Boski's conflict between head and heart was so severe that she deliberately overdosed on morphine in the early spring. Antheil, guilt stricken, took the near suicide for a sign he should quit concertizing and begin full-time composing. When Boski was back on her feet, he pledged himself to her and proposed they move to Paris and live together.

They did not move immediately. Antheil had several more concert engagements to fulfill, money in the bank. Across the spring he also found time to write a sonata he called *Death of Machines* and another, for his new love, called *Sonata Sauvage*. "When I later played it in Paris," he writes, "[it] caused a riot; if one may consider music able to represent anything visual, one might poetically consider that it was a portrait of her . . . because I habitually visualized her as a Mongolian-Hungarian amazon riding over an ancient 'pusta' full tilt." *Pusta* in Hungarian means plain, a broad grassland like the buffalo plains of North America. Boski was petite for an Amazon, barely five feet tall.

———

"We arrived in Paris in the middle of June," she remembered, "and the first night we were there, we went to the Theatre Sarah Bernhardt to see and hear the Diaghilev ballet performing Stravinsky's *Les noces*. What a magical beginning." *Les noces—The Wedding*—had given Stravinsky great trouble. He put the libretto together himself, mining a collection of old Russian wedding songs. Conceiving a dance cantata—a ballet with song—he originally tried to score it for full orchestra, "which I gave up almost at once in view of the elaborate apparatus that the complexity of the form demanded." Next he tried a smaller ensemble. "I began a score which required massed polyphonic effects: a mechanical piano and an electrically driven harmonium, a section of percussion instruments, and two Hungarian cimbaloms [that is, concert hammered dulcimers]." He worried that it would be difficult to synchronize the mechanical instruments with singers and the instruments played live by musicians. To see if the combination worked, he orchestrated the first two scenes. He was unhappy with the result; it "was all pure loss," he said, and he "did not touch *Les noces* again for four years." When Diaghilev asked for a new ballet for his Paris-based Ballets Russes, Stravinsky resuscitated *Les noces*, this time instrumenting it for multiple pianos, timbals, bells, and xylophones, "none of which instruments gives a precise note." Vaslav Nijinsky's sister, Bronislava, choreographed it. ("In contrast to her brother," Stravinsky writes acidly in his 1936 *Autobiography*, she was "gifted with a real talent for choreographic creation.") *Les noces* was performed that June 1923 to great acclaim. "Absolutely breathtaking," Boski praised it, "and the glitter and joyousness of the audience, after bleak Berlin, was like champagne."

Not only Berlin but also Vienna had been bleak. The war may not have affected Hedy Kiesler and her prosperous family; Boski, who had attended school in Vienna before beginning her university studies in Berlin, remembered an uglier reality. "When I went to school there," she writes, "after the First World War, Vienna and Austria were really terribly beaten, losing the war, losing their emperor, losing the illusion that they were the center of the universe. They were terribly poor, everything was rationed, and you had to wait in line for the simplest necessities of life."

Boski found Paris transforming:

Paris was like a carnival. I will never forget its busy ebullience on the early morning of our arrival: shops opened, housewives wearing slippers marketing, carrying shopping baskets for bread and milk, carts full of vegetables, noise, bustling, cheerful, sunny. We fell in love with it that instant . . . even though I was not too sure whether I had made the right decision coming to Paris with George. Not because it was "improper," for we in our generation tried to kick over the conventional ideas. I was quite radically minded, quite believing in woman's equal rights, fiercely believing in independence of spirit . . . and also slightly cynical about the world. . . . But George and Paris humanized me. I suddenly knew that just simply living can be fun.

Their first task was locating a place to live. Instead of consulting a realtor, they found Shakespeare and Company, Sylvia Beach's bookstore at 12, rue de l'Odéon on the Left Bank near the Luxembourg Gardens. "I still don't remember how we ever did get to Sylvia Beach's bookshop in the first place," Boski reminisced, "except that somehow within a week or two almost anyone interested or active in the arts did get to Shakespeare & Co."

Sylvia Beach, the daughter of the pastor of the First Presbyterian Church of Princeton, New Jersey, had opened her bookstore in Paris at a different location in 1919 after serving with the Red Cross in Serbia during the Great War. She moved to the larger rue de l'Odéon location in 1921. An English and American expatriate community formed in Paris in the 1920s in response to a highly favorable exchange rate and a conviction like Antheil's among artists and writers that their work would find more support abroad than at home. Perhaps because Beach maintained a rental library of books as well as sold them, perhaps because of her sympathy for struggling artists and writers—"she was kind, cheerful and interested, and loved to make jokes and gossip," Ernest Hemingway remembered of her—her bookstore became the expatriate community's lively center.

Besides Shakespeare and Company, Beach's greatest contribution to the literary life of the day was undertaking to publish James Joyce's controversial masterpiece *Ulysses*. She did so after the work had lost its American publisher. B. W. Huebsch, she wrote to a friend in 1921, "threw up the job in a fright" when an issue of the Greenwich Village journal the *Little Review* featuring a section of the book was declared obscene. Beach stepped in to save it, borrowing money from her family to publish it by subscription in Paris in regular and deluxe editions.

She had less luck locating a place for the Joyce family to live near Shakespeare and Company. "I tried my best to find an apartment for the Joyces," she told their mutual friend Harriet Weaver, "but as they required six rooms at least and as Mr. Joyce insisted on being in the Odéon quarter or very near it, there was nothing that could be done. There is never an apartment to be had in this quarter and excepting some impossible streets far from the center there is nothing on the entire Left Bank."

That hardly boded well for the newly arrived young lovers. "Sylvia and George immediately took a shine to each other," however, Boski recalled, "not only because George was American, not only because Sylvia was interested in every kind of artistic endeavor . . . but also because George was a Trentonian (even though a refugee of, as Sylvia was a refugee of Princeton) and their vocabulary, their physical landscape of youth was the same." Beach may have had an ulterior motive as well for helping Antheil; according to Bravig Imbs, another American expatriate who became a friend of the Antheils, the bookseller "was on the look-out for a talented composer, of course, having vague musical plans for James Joyce, and she intuitively recognized George's sincerity and force." If there was no apartment nearby for a family that required six rooms, there was an enclosed mezzanine directly above Beach's bookstore—she had been using it as a storeroom—that might suit a young couple traveling light. Boski remembered that it "consisted of one room with a so-called *cabinet de toilette* with a washbasin and shelves for dishes and a gas ring. It was a heavenly place as far as we were concerned." In those days, she said, "one went to the public baths, being careful to take along a bottle of Lysol, one's own towels and a warm overcoat to wear when one got out of the hot bath."

The Antheils, as they came to be, lived above Shakespeare and Company for more than ten years, expanding into two adjacent rooms when the American students to whom Beach rented them finished their studies and moved on. "George was a voracious reader," Boski said, "he was a voracious worker too, and apart from our friendship with Sylvia, it was wonderful to be able to go downstairs and borrow any amount of books and exchange them at a moment's notice. It helped me to learn English also." George pointed her to detective stories, on the theory that searching out the clues hidden in the story would encourage her to use the dictionary to look up any unfamiliar words. "I was very shy about my not knowing English and I was the most taciturn little thing for over a year until I finally ventured to say a few words in English. I am sure a lot of George's friends (who did not speak French which I spoke well) were surprised that the little Hungarian savage could talk."

After attending the *Les noces* premiere on the night they arrived in Paris, 13 June 1923, George and Boski had gone backstage to congratulate Stravinsky on his new ballet. The Russian composer had invited them to visit him the next day at Pleyel's, which Antheil calls "the great piano warehouse rooms where Chopin had often practiced." Pleyel was an old-line piano manufacturer, the French counterpart to Steinway or Bösendorfer. Besides making concert pianos, Pleyel manufactured player pianos—the firm, punning on its name, called its model a Pleyela.

Player pianos, the entertainment centers of their day, brought music into homes in the half century before radio replaced them with a full menu of music and voice transmissions. The great advantage of the player piano was that it did not require piano lessons or years of practice to play, merely legs strong enough to pump the bellows that supplied the vacuum to actuate the works. The first player pianos had been cabinet players—Americans called them push-ups—large wooden cabinets that hunched over the keyboards of standard pianos and actually pressed the piano keys with felt-covered mechanical wooden fingers. Gradually, piano owners parted with their standard pianos and push-ups and replaced them with player pianos, which had internal mechanical workings, could be played mechanically or by hand, and took up much less space. By 1919, player pianos had become so popular in Europe and America that their production outnumbered the production of standard pianos.

Music to be performed on a player piano was recorded on a roll of tough paper. Technicians cut holes and slots into the paper roll by hand, following the notations on the sheet music. In operation, the roll was loaded onto spools in the player piano much as recording tape is wound reel to reel. Pumping the pedals then scrolled the punched paper over a row of vacuum ducts—small holes, one for each piano key, in a brass bar called a tracker bar that looked much like an extremely long harmonica. The spooling paper covered the tracker ducts, holding the mechanism behind them at rest, until a hole or slot in the paper allowed air to be sucked into the duct. A rubber tube connected the tracker duct to one of a series of valve chests. The air flowing from the tube into the valve chest activated a sequence of valves and bladders that drove up a pushrod that in turn actuated the piano key.

The piano rolls cut by hand following sheet music notations reproduced music purely mechanically; they did not program changes in tempo or dynamics. Player-piano operators had to adjust these qualities in real time, pumping more or less vigorously and manipulating a tempo lever. Some piano rolls featured a printed expression line that wavered up or down as the roll turned to direct the player's adjustments. These adaptations distracted from listening and still failed to reproduce an authentic professional performance.

To improve the quality of recordings, manufacturers developed reproducing pianos with electric motors to drive the pneumatics, up to sixteen dynamic levels between soft and loud, and multitrack piano rolls that could register and generate the variations. It then became possible for a pianist or composer to record a musical work with some confidence that its player-piano reproduction would approximate his performance.

Pleyel had contacted Stravinsky in 1921 to propose that he transcribe his works for the Pleyela reproducing piano. The company offered him the use of a suite of rooms in its building in Paris and technical support. He quickly decided to accept the offer, he wrote, for two reasons:

> In order to prevent the distortion of my compositions
> by future interpreters, I had always been anxious to find
> a means of imposing some restriction on the notorious
> liberty . . . which prevents the public from obtaining
> a correct idea of the author's intentions. This possibil-
> ity was now afforded by the rolls of the mechanical
> piano. . . .
> There was a second direction in which this work

gave me satisfaction. This was not simply the reduction of an orchestral work to the limitations of a piano of seven octaves. It was the process of adaptation to an instrument which had, on the one hand, unlimited possibilities of precision, velocity, and polyphony, but which, on the other hand, constantly presented serious difficulties in establishing dynamic relationships. These tasks developed and exercised my imagination.

After the *Les noces* premiere, Antheil recalled, "the next day we went to see him at Pleyel's . . . and Stravinsky himself played *Les noces*, this time on an electric pianola. I liked the second version even better than the one which we had heard last night; it was more precise, colder, harder, more typical of that which I myself wanted out of music during this period of my life." He told Stravinsky it was wonderful. Boski concurred.

A day or two later, abruptly, Stravinsky dropped him, refused his calls, made no answer to an inquiring letter. Antheil learned from a mutual friend that the composer had taken umbrage over reports that Antheil had claimed they were close friends, that Stravinsky admired his music, and that the two had spent all their time together in Berlin. "Months later I encountered him at a concert," Antheil writes ruefully, "but his steely monocle bored straight through me." The two friends did not reconnect for more than a decade.

The incident depressed Antheil "tremendously," he

recalled. "It haunted my dreams for many years." No doubt it did, but Boski believed it also released him from his hero worship of the older man. "I'm happy about it!" she told him. "You liked Stravinsky's music too much." Stravinsky's abrupt rejection motivated Antheil to compete with his former hero—"for where," he writes, "is the younger man who does not revolt against his elders?" And, a little later, speaking as if for his whole generation: "We are done with [Erik] Satie, Les Six, Stravinsky, and the Dadaists. Even though we recognize the value of the innovations brought about by these men in our imbecilic age, we want nothing to do with them."

As one mentor pulled away, another almost immediately stepped forward. The American poet Ezra Pound, introduced to Antheil by a mutual friend, "turned up . . . in a green coat with blue square buttons; and his red pointed goatee and kinky red hair above flew off his face in all directions. Boski looked at him, not a little astonished." Antheil played several hours' worth of his compositions for the Pennsylvania expatriate and shared his theories of the future of music, after which Pound decided to write a short, flamboyant book about the man, *Antheil and the Treatise on Harmony*.

While working on his book, Pound moved to promote his latest protégée, who happened also to be his mistress, the American violinist Olga Rudge. "A dark, pretty, Irish-looking girl," Antheil recalled her, twenty-eight years old in 1923, "and, as I discovered when we commenced playing a Mozart sonata together, a consummate violinist." Pound wanted to arrange a concert for Rudge and Antheil. "At this concert, he explained, he would take care to see that all of important Paris was present, the really important Paris that mattered." To that end, he wanted his friend to compose for Rudge not one but *two* violin sonatas.

Antheil's solution to the problem of composing two violin sonatas in a matter of months—it was the end of July, and the concert would be scheduled for November—was to swoop Boski up and take her off to Tunis, on the north coast of Africa opposite Sicily. They both liked the fierce heat of North African summer. They remained in Tunis for a month, listening to Arabic music that Antheil copied down with his phonographic ear while writing not a note of his own.

Because he was vacationing in Tunis that August, Antheil was not in Paris when two sometime American filmmakers, Man Ray and Dudley Murphy, began shooting clips for an art film. Murphy had seen Man Ray's work at a Dada theater gathering, *Le coeur à barbe* (*The Bearded Heart*), on 6 July 1923. (Antheil may have attended as well; he left for Tunis later in July.) The event included premieres of compositions by Stravinsky, Satie, and Darius Milhaud; poems; a Tristan Tzara play (named for another heart, this one gas: *Le coeur à gaz*); and several short films, including Man Ray's first, *Le retour à la raison* (*The Return to Reason*), a three-minute silent, semiabstract short. "All the celebrities of Paris," the *Little Review*'s publisher, Jane Heap, writes, "painters, sculptors, musicians, poets; foreigners of every title, and rich excitement-hunting Americans turned out for this ultra-modern show." Fights broke out. "Canes clashed, mirrors and footlights smashed, the audience stamped and laughed and shouted."

Some time after the Dada gathering, Dudley Murphy paid Man Ray a visit. "One day a tall young man appeared with his beautiful blond wife," Man Ray recalled. "Dudley Murphy said some very flattering things about my work and suggested we do a film together." Murphy was the son of a prominent Boston School painter, Hermann Dudley Murphy, who taught drawing at Harvard. Young Murphy's parents had divorced when he was a teenager, and he had moved with his mother to Pasadena. He had grown up with the movie business at a time when Hollywood was still tolerant of experimental film work. He arrived in Paris in 1923 an accomplished director with one feature and numerous short art films to his credit.

Who precisely was responsible for the now-classic art film *Ballet mécanique* has been a subject of debate for more than eighty years. Murphy and Man Ray evidently contributed more mise-en-scène and footage than the French artist Fernand Léger, to whom the film is usually credited. What no one disputes is that Antheil signed on later in 1923 to write the film score and produced a score that was twice as long as the film and never cut or synced to fit. Boski's recollection of the informality of the film's production is probably as accurate as any. "Even though the idea of the film and music called *Ballet mécanique* was to be a joint conception of Léger, Dudley Murphy and George," she writes, "it seems to me everyone, in their individual manner, went their own way. George got so enthused about composing the music that any synchronization between objects of the film and tone clusters and tempo of music must be considered purely coincidental. But this was nothing that bothered us in those days, things didn't have to 'fit' as they do in commercial pictures, as long as essentially they had an esthetic connection."

Before Antheil could begin work on the film music, he wrote Rudge's two sonatas and practiced them extensively with her. Margaret Anderson, Jane Heap's partner and the editor of the *Little Review,* invited him to perform on the opening program of the Ballets Suédois—the Swedish Ballet company—on 4 October 1923. Antheil knew the occasion was second in importance only to the Ballets Russes as an annual Parisian cultural event. He signed on to play several of his recent compositions: the *Sonata Sauvage*, his *Airplane* Sonata, a two-minute, four-movement sonatina called *Death of Machines*, and his *Mechanisms*, composed for the player piano. ("George was writing his *Mechanisms* for a hard new age," Boski recalled of its composition the previous year, "and I still remember his talking about the future when one central recording station would be blasting talks [and] music over a whole city.")

In his memoirs Antheil would present the riot that broke

out during his Ballets Suédois concert as spontaneous, but in fact it had been set up by another Parisian filmmaker, Marcel L'Herbier, to create a scene for a film he was making, *L'inhumaine*, which showcased the French opera singer Georgette Leblanc. Sylvia Beach's partner, Adrienne Monnier, confirms that Antheil had not been informed in advance that he was intended to bait a riot: "Georgette Leblanc, back from America, knew through her friend Margaret Anderson that Antheil's music always caused a scandal; and if it caused a scandal in New York, what was it going to be like in Paris! . . . Antheil had believed that they had seriously asked him to play his most 'advanced' music; when he saw the trick, he was not angry, he had a lot of fun." L'Herbier had sent out several thousand concert invitations to notable Parisians. As a result, Antheil writes, "the theater, the famous Champs Elysees Theater, was crowded with the most famous personages of the day, among others Picasso, Stravinsky, [the French composer Georges] Auric, Milhaud, James Joyce, Erik Satie, Man Ray, Diaghileff, Miró, Arthur Rubenstein, Ford Madox Ford, and unnumbered others. They had not come to hear me, but to see the opening of the ballets."

They heard very little. "The uproar was such," Boski said, "that after [George] started to play one of his 'mechanisms' nobody could really hear very much. . . . The riot was tremendous. Not being George's wife officially, I was seated way up in the balcony and was really scared, when people started to throw things and screaming and yelling, that they might hurt George. But he was used to this and kept on playing as cool as can be. He seemed too slight and almost childlike, calmly playing the piano, not paying the slightest attention to all the commotion." Antheil registered the fighting around him but managed to hear what he hoped to hear as well:

I now plunged into my "Mechanisms." Then bedlam really did break loose. People now punched one another freely. Nobody remained in his seat. One wave of persons seemed about to break over the other wave. That's the way a riot commences, one wave over the other. People were fighting in the aisles, yelling, clapping, hooting! Pandemonium!

I suddenly heard Satie's shrill voice saying, "*Quelle precision! Quelle precision!* [What precision!] Bravo! Bravo!" And he kept clapping his little gloved hands. Milhaud now was clapping, definitely clapping.

By this time some people in the galleries were pulling up the seats and dropping them down into the orchestra; the police entered, and any number of surrealists, society personages, and people of all descriptions were arrested.

I finished the "Mechanisms" as calm as a cucumber.

Paris hadn't had such a good time since the premiere of Stravinsky's "Sacre du Printemps." As Jack Benny would have said: "Boy, they loved me in Paris!"

A contemporary reviewer reveals that Antheil's version of
the riot leaves out a restaging that was called for L'Herbier's
film:

> After the finish of the first movement of the "sonata"
> the Champs-Elysees was the scene of the greatest
> musical riot since the performance of the "Sacre du
> Printemps" eleven years ago. After the first movement
> no one heard a note, except in the infrequent lulls: The
> audience shouted itself quite hoarse with both indigna-
> tion with the composer and indignation with the others
> in the audience who prevented them from hearing. . . .
> [Then] the master of ceremonies came out to
> announce that motion pictures would now be taken of
> the audience, and would they be so kind as to repro-
> duce the riot which had just taken place when Monsieur
> Antheil had played. The audience, in a fighting spirit,
> was so kind, with the result that many famous faces
> were immortalized behind clapping and enthusiastic
> hands—those whose approval it is hardest to earn.

The scene of staged riot duly appeared the following year in
L'Herbier's film. Antheil accomplished his purpose as well.
"Satie came out in my favor, and, as he and Cocteau were
then the artistic arbitrators of Paris, I was famous overnight."

There remained his concert with Olga Rudge, which was
held at the Salle du Conservatoire in Paris's 9th arrondisse-

ment on 11 December 1923. This event was probably the occasion that Aaron Copland recalled "where Antheil played, and Ezra Pound, with his striking red beard much in evidence, passionately turned pages."

And then, finally, Antheil was free to spend the rest of the winter and spring composing the music for *Ballet mécanique*, except that by then it had enlarged in his mind beyond a film score into a showpiece. "My first big work," he wrote to a childhood friend. "Scored for countless numbers of player pianos. All percussive. Like machines. All efficiency. NO LOVE. Written without sympathy. Written cold as an army operates. Revolutionary as nothing has been revolutionary."

[T H R E E]

Mechanisms

The film *Ballet mécanique* premiered in Vienna on 24 September 1924, without George Antheil's music. As late as March 1926, when the film was screened at the London Film Society, a note in the program apologized for the missing soundtrack: "Mr. George Antheil was engaged in the composition of music for this picture but, according to Mr. Léger, his music is not likely to be suitably ready for some time and a jazz accompaniment suggested by Mr. Léger will accordingly be played instead." The music was written by then—Antheil recalled composing the greater part of it "during the winter of 1923–24"—but it had grown from a film score into a major composition. "The work had really sprung from previous inspiration," Antheil explained, "derived from its three predecessors: the 'Sonata Sauvage,' the 'Airplane Sonata,' and the 'Mechanisms'—to say nothing of my microscopic sonatina, 'Death of Machines.' But it was a work of greater length

57

and orchestration; it also said more exactly what I wanted to say in this medium."

Nor was Antheil himself present for the film's 1924 Viennese premiere; had he been, he would have advanced one move closer to Hedy Kiesler, because the organizer of the premiere at the International Exhibition of New Theater Techniques of the City of Vienna Music and Theater Festival was an architect and set designer named Frederick Kiesler, who happened to be a relative. Hedy herself was not quite ten years old in September 1924, probably too young to have seen the film. Léger lectured on it and presented it.

George and Boski did meet Frederick Kiesler a year later in Paris at the 1925 Exposition of Decorative Arts. Boski remarked on their affinities:

> Kiesler liked it so well in Paris that he decided to stay there after the Exposition and we became very good friends. He had a most original way of communicating in French, as at the time he did not speak it. When we went to restaurants, he just drew pictures of things he wanted to eat and was never disappointed. He loved the *Ballet mécanique*, which represented the same ideology as his architecture, and we saw a lot of each other. He had a very nice Austrian wife. Kiesler was very short and hence somewhat Napoleonic in his bearing. But he knew the humor of it and was delighted when we photographed him in a typical Napoleonic pose.

Kiesler stood only four feet eleven inches tall, which would have recommended him to George and Boski but must have contrasted conspicuously with Hedy's tall father, Emil. George and Boski took time out in 1925 to marry, in Budapest on 4 November. Boski had been away from Hungary long enough to notice how her native language colored even American song lyrics. "One night we went to a gypsy restaurant," she recalled, "where they played a lot of Magyar songs, but eventually they got around to playing their versions of popular American hits, one of them being 'Tea for Two,' but you would never know it. It sounded exactly like a Hungarian folk song from the 'pusta' with cimbalom accompaniment."

Another of the Antheils' acquaintances in Paris whom they would encounter again significantly in the United States was William C. Bullitt, the journalist and diplomat, thirty-four years old in 1925. In 1933, Bullitt would become the first U.S. ambassador to the Soviet Union, traveling there with a young interpreter and diplomatic secretary named George Kennan. "Bullitt is a striking man," Kennan would recall: "young, handsome, urbane, full of charm and enthusiasm, a product of Philadelphia society and Yale but with considerable European residence, and with a flamboyance of personality that is right out of F. Scott Fitzgerald." (Antheil's young American acquaintance Bravig Imbs took a less diplomatic view of the man when he encountered him in 1926; he described Bullitt as "a hearty, charming and slightly silly gentleman who lived in a magnificent house near the Madeleine.") The Philadelphian was moderately wealthy, with an inheritance from his mother that would be the equivalent of about $750,000 today. He had served as an assistant to President Woodrow Wilson at the Paris Peace Conference following the Great War. With the American journalist Lincoln Steffens he had traveled on a secret mission to Russia during the conference and returned with an offer from Lenin of a peace treaty, an offer that Wilson had rejected. In his bitterness over the failure of his mission and the punitive harshness of the Versailles Treaty that followed, he had quit politics in disgust.

By 1925, settled in Paris and finishing a satiric novel about Philadelphia society, Bullitt had transformed his life from that of a diplomat into that of a writer and wealthy expatriate. His second wife, whom he had married in 1923, was the former Louise Bryant, the widow of John Reed. Both Bryant and Reed had experienced and written books about the Russian Revolution, Reed's *Ten Days That Shook the World* the better known of the two. Reed had died of typhus in 1920. He was the only American buried beneath the Kremlin Wall, the necropolis of Soviet national honor.

Boski remarks on the tension between the Bullitts in her unpublished memoir:

> And of course there was Bill Bullitt and his beautiful wife Louise, who could never get over her guilt feeling of having married a millionaire (no matter how much she loved him) after having been married to

John Reed. Who died in Russia and was buried before
Louise got there by special Russian dispensation, as in
those days there was no such traveling there and it was
very much a closed country. The only American hero
of the revolution was John Reed, who shared the high-
est respect with the top Russian revolutionaries. Bullitt
was special envoy to Russia at the time, and met Louise
there, fell in love with her and eventually married her.
[When we knew him in Paris] he was in a period of
deep disillusionment about politics and said at the time
that he never wants to have anything to do with it.
Instead they both turned to the art world of Paris and
had some fabulous, but rather off-beat, parties at their
elegant mansion. Louise was a beautiful woman, but
you felt that she was a tragic woman, ambivalent about
herself.

Bullitt was politically liberal but culturally conservative,
not someone likely to have felt an affinity with Antheil's
music. During Louise's pregnancy, Steffens had read aloud
to her in Bullitt's absence one evening from Joyce's *Ulysses*;
when Bullitt arrived home and took in the situation, Steffens's
wife recalled, "He was furious. He bellowed at Steff: 'Think
of our baby, our child! What will it turn out to be if it hears
language like that?'" Bullitt may have been sensitized to the
imagined dangers of uterine imprinting by his ongoing psychoanalysis with another Vienna denizen, Sigmund Freud;

several years later he and Freud would collaborate on a joint psychoanalytic study of Woodrow Wilson, although Freud had never met the president and Bullitt was not a psychoanalyst.

Despite these strains, or perhaps because of them, the Bullitts gave great parties, Boski recalled:

> Bill and Louise . . . had a very interesting conglomeration of people at their parties, down-and-out artists, French aristocracy, successful artists, American upper four hundred, etc. Louise had the most fabulous gowns from the great designers and she held these magnificent dresses in such low esteem that often, I remember, if her dress had a long train, we would use it to jump rope. . . . It's hard to explain how elegant these parties were, with butlers galore, absolutely phenomenal food, Louise in her Vionnet dress, Bill in tuxedo, most women in long dresses or else very artistic confections of artists' wives who had little money but a lot of imagination.

"We had a lovely and lively time that summer," Boski writes elsewhere. "All summer was a marvelous fair. George was getting the *Ballet mécanique* ready and the *rouleaux* were being cut at Pleyel and we used to go there with friends who wanted to hear it 'in progress.' " The *rouleaux* were the paper player-piano rolls. "[*Ballet mécanique*] was very hard to play, because there were so many notes that one had to pump the pedal very hard in order to get all the notes to sound. It was written directly to be cut into the pianola roll."

Writing in a prophetic mood in one of the manifestos George published during this period in avant-garde periodicals like the Dutch art journal *De Stijl*—as time went on, he would prove to be gifted at prophecy—he encapsulated the giddy, febrile Paris mood in a phrase. "One day in the future," he wrote, "we will make God in the heavens with electric lights."

Boski remembered fondly the Vienna of the late 1920s, where Hedy was dropping out of school and preparing to storm the film studio barricades and where they crossed paths again without meeting:

We went to Vienna for George to finish [an] opera there. We had quite a wonderful time in Vienna which I don't believe was ever as charming as in the late twenties. Finances were better, people were happily indolent, enjoying themselves. We had an apartment in the Prater Strasse, not a fashionable district, but very comfortable and near the Prater [city park]. We more or less introduced our Austrian friends to a game called poker, which they took up with great enthusiasm. . . . They finally got so good that we had to watch our step. They were composers, writers, executives of Universal Verlag, then the most influential publishing house in Europe. Everybody was very young, mostly under thirty and full of enthusiasm.

. . . We went to the opera or concerts practically every night.

But darkness was drifting across Germany and beginning to spill into Austria, and Fritz Mandl rode the black wave. "Fritz was immersed in the family arms business," *Time* would report of Hedy's husband-to-be. "His firm had a sharp reputation for circumventing the restrictions of the Allied Control Commissions. His own politics were opportunistic. . . . He backed Prince Ernst Rüdiger von Starhemberg and his fascist Home Guard [and] bet on [the Austrofascist federal chancellor Engelbert] Dollfuss and [the Italian dictator Benito] Mussolini to stave off Hitler." The politics of postwar Austria, a historian writes, "are unintelligible except to a virtuoso," but it's clear at least that Mandl's politics lined his pockets; Hirtenberger arms would rearm Austria and Germany and fuel the Italian slaughter of Ethiopians in that 1935–36 colonialist excursion.

The high point of George Antheil's musical career, much to his enduring chagrin, was the grand public premiere of his *Ballet mécanique*—the freestanding composition, not the film theme music—in Paris in the twenty-five-hundred-seat Théâtre des Champs-Élysées on 19 June 1926. With his patron's substantial support Antheil hired the French conductor Vladimir Golschmann, who conducted for the Ballets Russes, eighty-five musicians, and Paris's largest concert hall. "The only serious problem," writes one of Antheil's biographers, "was a score that called for sixteen mechanical pianos, all to be operated by cables attached to a master keyboard. It is doubtful if that many [player] pianos existed in all of France, and even if they did, bringing them together on one stage would have been a daunting task. [As an alternative] Antheil assembled eight grand pianos, engaged eight players, and wired up an amplifier to the master piano he would operate. As for the nonmusical instruments the score required, local hardware stores supplied saws, hammers, and electric bells; and from a flea market came two airplane propellers that would help bring the *Ballet* to a noisy and windy climax."

Some have questioned if Antheil actually intended his composition to include sixteen synchronized player pianos or was only exaggerating for effect. A letter to Mrs. Bok, his patron, accompanying a copy of the Pianola score, which he sent her in December 1925, settles the question in favor of the full complement of pianos. "This is the first edition of the *Ballet mécanique*," Antheil wrote, "and is limited to 20 copies. It is the *16-pianola part alone*, none of the xylophones, drums, and other percussion being written into or cut into *this* part. These are the master rolls which run the 16 pianolas electrically from a common control (switching on 16 or 1, as might be necessary to the sonority) together with which the other percussion is synchronized."

Synchronizing the player pianos electrically might have solved the problem, but no such control system existed at the time. The "cables" of Antheil's biographer isn't right either. A nonelectrical system would have required elaborate pneumatics worthy of a mighty pipe organ, which was not something that could be assembled at relatively short notice for a concert. Antheil explained many years afterward that the essential problem was getting enough fortissimo out of the piano part. "The idea of [sixteen] pianos," he wrote in 1951, "had been to swell or amplify the original [part] when 'fff' was desirable; today the same effect may be had through four pianos and one microphone." He solved the problem in 1926 by using eight grand pianos played by eight pianists who could be directed to play in synchrony; the synchronization mechanism was thus the human brain.

The Théâtre des Champs-Élysées concert, on a sweltering June evening, was one of the touchstone events of the 1920s in Paris. Ezra Pound had marshaled all his forces. Among those who filled the large hall were James and Nora Joyce and their two children; tall, top-hatted T. S. Eliot with the Princess di Bassiano; the wealthy salonist Natalie Barney with her temple of friendships; Diaghilev; Constantin Brancusi; the Boston Symphony Orchestra conductor Serge Koussevitzky; Sylvia Beach and Adrienne Monnier; the Russian sculptor Ossip Zadkine; the writers William L. Shirer and Stuart Gilbert; Antheil's unbathed and somewhat unhinged Philadelphia friend Lincoln Gillespie; the French poet Pierre Minet;

the Antheils' concierge, Madame Tisserand, looking like a duchess in a black dress with a face powdered white with bread flour and seated next to a real one, the Duchesse de Clermont-Tonnerre; Man Ray and his mistress, Alice Prin, better known as Kiki of Montparnasse, the woman whose iconic face centered Léger's film; and many, many more. Of several eyewitness accounts of the *Ballet mécanique* portion of the concert, that of Antheil's droll protégé Bravig Imbs is unsurpassed:

> There was a great deal of fuss while the orchestra arranged itself for this event. George appeared on the stage, pale and nervous, giving crisp directions to the movers who were pushing five pianos into place, and to the electricians who were arranging a loud-speaker to amplify the small electric fans that took the place of the airplane propellers. All these operations variously provoked fear, pity and amusement in the audience. Finally, George nodded his head, as a cue to Golschmann that everything was ready, and sat down at his piano with a grim expression on his face.
>
> Within a few minutes, the concert became sheer bedlam. Above the mighty noise of the pianos and drums arose cat-calls and booing, shrieking and whistling, shouts of "thief" mixed with "bravo." People began to call each other names and to forget that there was any music going on at all. I suffered with George, wish-

ing that people would have at least the courtesy to stay quiet, but Golschmann was so furious he would not give up his baton, and continued to conduct imperturbably as though he were the dead centre of a whirlpool.

I caught the general fever of unrest myself.

"Do keep quiet, please," I said to some of my particularly noisy neighbors.

"Shut your face, yourself," they answered, and then started whistling, which is the supreme form of contempt in France.

Then, for an instant, there was a curious lull in the clamor and Ezra Pound took advantage of it to jump to his feet and yell, "*Vous etes tous des imbéciles!*"

He was shouted down from the gallery, of course, with many vulgar epithets, and the music continued monotonously and determinedly.

The *Ballet* began to seem to me like some monstrous abstract beast, battling with the nerves of the audience, and I began to wonder which would win out. . . .

The opposition reached its climax, though, when the loud-speaker began to function. It made as much noise as a dozen airplanes, and no amount of shouting could drown it completely. One fat bald old gentleman who had been particularly disagreeable would not be balked by this, however, and to the glee of the audience, lashed out his umbrella, opened it and pretended to be struggling against the imaginary gale of wind from the electric fans. His gesture was immediately copied by many more people in the audience until the theatre seemed decked with quite a sprinkling of black mushrooms.

Of course, when the *Ballet* was over, George got an ovation which was greater than the cat-calls, for everyone was willing to applaud a man who had at least accomplished something. He bowed and blushed and blushed and bowed and all his friends were very proud of him.

In the "Manifest der Musico-Mechanico" he published in *De Stijl* in 1924 (but wrote in Berlin in 1922), Antheil had envisioned a future music enriched with new sonics through the use of mechanical reproduction, a prediction that his experiments with synchronized multiple instruments and player-piano technology would encourage and support:

We shall see orchestral machines with a thousand new sounds, with thousands of new euphonies, as opposed to the present day's simple sounds of strings, brass, and woodwinds. It is only a short step until all [musical performance] can be perforated onto a roll of paper. Of course, we will find sentimental people who will object that there will then be no more of these wonderful imprecisions in performance. But, dear friends, these can be added to the paper roll! Do not object; you can have what you want.

At that time the paper roll and the player piano were the most reliable mechanisms for accomplishing his ends. But the player piano, which had accounted for more than half of all pianos manufactured in the United States in 1919, was already in steep decline as the new technology of radio emerged to replace it, providing a far larger range of musical performances from an instrument that required no training or effort to operate. Five thousand radios sold in 1920 became 2.5 million sold in 1924; 30 radio stations in the United States in 1922 had become 606 radio stations in the United States by 1929. In 1932, with the disaster of the Great Depression, Americans bought only two thousand player pianos.

Player pianos might be obsolete. The player-piano roll, however, was an early system of digital control, like the punched-card control system of the early-nineteenth-century Jacquard loom from which it ultimately derived. Antheil did not forget its usefulness. "And what will the music of the future be?" he asked in an essay written in Tunis during the summer following the Paris *Ballet mécanique* performance. "It will be machinery . . . never fear that. But silent machinery, dreams, spaces which the heart cannot fill."

His *Ballet mécanique* encountered a far more hostile reception in New York in 1927 than it had in Paris in 1926. Donald Friede, a wealthy young American publisher who had the unusual distinction of having been thrown successively out of Harvard, Yale, and Princeton, invited Antheil to give a concert in Carnegie Hall, assumed all expenses, and assured

Antheil he would make a profit on the venture. Antheil agreed and arrived with Boski in March 1927 for the 10 April event. Boski was amazed at New York; it seemed to her both remote and ultramodern:

> When I first came to New York with George on that famous Ballet Mecanique outing, we were often taken to night clubs, speakeasies, to Harlem, all of which left me with a feeling of a fascinating, rather savage land, an ancient Babylon projected into the future. The skyscrapers were like deep canyons, and New York had a particular, deep acrid smell, fanned by the wind from the river, steam heat coming out from underneath the pavement like so many fires and smoke coming from Hades. . . .
>
> I could not get over the "newness" of everything in N.Y. Furniture, rugs, entrance halls with doormen in elegant uniforms, the buildings all new (at least where we lived) and the smell of newness. Like tomorrow. It was really futuristic, at least the way some European artists visualized the cities of the future.

Friede, at twenty-five in 1927 a year younger than Antheil, was good at publicity and spared no expense. Ford Madox Ford wrote a profile of Antheil for *Vanity Fair*. Man Ray and Berenice Abbott photographed the heralded young composer. Miguel Covarrubias and William Cotton drew caricatures. James M. Cain, at that time an editorial writer for the New York *World*, panned the concert in advance, sight unseen, then reversed himself and praised it after meeting the Antheils and sitting through a rehearsal. "The eleven grand pianos," Friede writes—one for Antheil, ten for his slaved counterparts—"made a magnificent picture in the huge Welte-Mignon [piano] studios. . . . Even the mechanical problems proved to be not too difficult. We found an electrician who undertook to make the battery of electric bells that we needed. We commissioned a wind machine with a regulation airplane propeller. And we started our search for a real fire siren." They had more difficulty with the *Jazz Symphony*, since it turned out that the pianist and conductor W. C. Handy couldn't read an orchestra score.

The concert sold out within twenty-four hours of its announcement. "Everybody wanted to meet Antheil," Friede notes, which meant almost nightly parties during the Antheils' entire stay in New York. The most memorable, says Friede, was at "Theodore Dreiser's enormous studio on Fifty-seventh Street," where Dreiser pumped Antheil dry of information about his music and his life. More intimately, a Harlem choir led by the composer and choirmaster Hall Johnson crowded into Friede's apartment one evening and sang spirituals until guests and chorus both were exhausted.

Unintentionally, Friede had paved the way for disaster with all his publicity. "The trouble was that I was doing for a musical event what I would normally do for a book. And I did not realize that one by one I was alienating all the critics, all the people who were really important to [Antheil], all the people who had contributed toward making it possible for him to write his music without any financial worries, by turning a serious performance into a circus."

The performance itself, on a Sunday evening, *was* something of a circus. The real airplane propeller in use in the performance had been aimed downstage, directly at the audience, instead of upstage, where the blast of air it generated could collide and disperse. "When it reached full power," writes Friede, "it was disastrous. People clutched their programs, and women held onto their hats with both hands. Someone in the direct line of the wind tied a handkerchief to his cane and waved it wildly in the air in a sign of surrender." The percussionist quickly slowed the motor, "but the damage had been done. Laughter is contagious, and besides we had spent weeks building up the fact that there had been riots in Paris at the first performance of this number. Now everybody . . . wanted to get into the act. The riot they put on, however, was completely synthetic. [The conductor] turned to glare at the noisemakers, and they shut up at once. Then the more conservative members of the audience decided that they had had enough. They started to leave in droves. It was an agonizing experience for Antheil, and I, back in my box once more, could not help but feel for him. I knew he wished, as I did most fervently, that we had never heard of each other."

Antheil was devastated, not least because of the reports he knew Mrs. Bok would hear and read. He wrote to her the next day, mentioning a second concert scheduled for Wednesday that was nearly sold out as well. "The unheard-of viciousness of the critical press," he warned his patron, "which even went as far as prevarication in minimizing even the scandal of the performance, which was a great one . . . has earned me . . . no doubt justly from their viewpoint . . . the suspicion of the concert agencies, and scotched for the moment my return to America this autumn under any except circus auspices." He had, he said, "no prospect except that of a sticky summer in Paris as a recreation from all this rehearsing, hatreds, ridicule, strain of appearing in public, etc. Worse, worse, worst of all there is no prospect now of my coming over in my piano concerto next season and earning some money. They do not want that . . . they want sensations, and I won't do it at any cost."

"This year I made two mistakes," he wrote to her further a few days later: "I came to America too soon, and I had played a program of my earliest and most sensational works. [Now] I am leaving America again as an exile, and my heart is indeed breaking this time." Of course he was seeking her support, and for a few more years she gave it.

Antheil sailed back to France with Boski and Friede before the end of April, he said, "heartsick and broke." By then, he had decided he was finished with the kind of music, time structured rather than tonal, that *Ballet mécanique* represented. In his 1945 memoir, *Bad Boy of Music*, he would move the end of that first phase of his compositional career back to 1924, when he completed *Ballet*, three years before the Carnegie Hall disaster. In a letter to Mrs. Bok just before he sailed, however, he announced the decision that he later backdated:

> America has received a blow . . . the length and viciousness . . . the absolutely unheard-of viciousness of the attacks of the critics . . . viewed from a distance is very enheartening. The Ballet Mecanique has floored them. Only yesterday a critic said that after the B.M. he cannot hear [the French-born American composer Edgard] Varèse anymore.
>
> The B.M. being the height, and best expression of the kind of thing that all the rest of these people are trying to do, automatically kills interest in all the rest of it, and puts a stop to the movement forever, for it can never never be repeated. In their day Sacre du Printemps and Tristan und Isolde were the high points of their day, and as their beauty (or ugliness, just as you wish, they are the same) could not be repeated in another work, it represented the height of its movement, and consequently is deceased. The Ballet Mecanique is the end of a period: one can stand upon one's head, or do what one likes, but it is there.

The timing of Antheil's new phase, and its presumably intentional backdating in his autobiography, suggest that his decision to compose more conventional music was influenced in part by the brutal New York reception of his *Ballet mécanique*. Whether or not that was so, across the next six years, living once again in Paris, Antheil continued to flourish musically. "I changed my musical style radically in 1927," he wrote in an autobiographical note some years later, "deciding upon a lyric style and the investigation of operatic possibilities. I embarked upon an opera, *Transatlantic*, which subsequently was accepted by the Frankfurter Opera a/M. and given there in May 1930. It was successful. I became involved in other theatrical productions, including music for a play, *Oedipus*, given at the Berlin Staatstheater, and another play, *Fighting the Waves*, by W. B. Yeats, given during this 1928–31 period at the Abbey Theatre in Dublin by Yeats himself." He wrote a second opera as well, *Helen Retires*; a Concert for Chamber Orchestra; his Second Symphony and Second String Quartet; and, augury of a parallel career to come, a pseudonymous crime novel, *Death in the Dark*, that T. S. Eliot, by then an editor at Faber and Faber, published. No one ever said George Antheil was lazy.

A Guggenheim Fellowship sustained the Antheils in 1932, but they saw the larger European disaster forming. They moved to the Riviera that summer and rented a beautiful house:

The place was well calculated to make one forget. The Riviera, in 1932, was a gorgeous soundproofed paradise, utterly oblivious of the darkness gathering over the rest of Europe. Here a synthetic sun shone on glittering synthetic beaches full of synthetically happy people. I said to myself, "I don't care. This will be the last fling before I leave Europe forever. In one, two, or five years there will be a war, after which the Europe I know will be no more. Excepting, of course, Paris—Paris will never, must never, perish. Paris sees only civilizations roll over and past her; she will forever remain the art city. But Europe, the Europe of my youth, it is finished for a long time. Here, then, the last orgies before the flood!"

Hitler's assumption of the German chancellorship on 30 January 1933 turned the tide. "He decides the handwriting's on the wall," Antheil recalled the moment in the third person, "two months later he's back in America to stay."

So an ocean separated George Antheil from Hedy Kiesler Mandl just as she, in Vienna, began to test the locks on her golden prison.

FOUR

Between Times

In the late 1920s, after he had revitalized his family's armaments business, Fritz Mandl began investing in Austrian right-wing politics. To advance his social status as well as his business interests, he cultivated in particular Prince Ernst Rüdiger Starhemberg, an heir to the defunct Austro-Hungarian throne who was a member of the Austrian parliament and a leader of the nationalist paramilitary *Heimatschutz* (Homeland Security) movement. Starhemberg, a year older than Mandl, had stood with Adolf Hitler in the Beer Hall Putsch in Munich in 1923; the putsch's failure put Hitler in prison and sent the disaffected prince back to Austria. By the end of the decade he had exhausted his family's wealth. Thereafter Mandl supported him to buy his influence.

Mandl and Starhemberg converted the *Heimatschutz* movement into a private militia, the *Heimwehr* (Home

Guard), which Mandl armed with surplus weapons shipped to Hirtenberger Patronen-Fabrik from Italy ostensibly to be reconditioned for the Hungarian army—as many as 100,000 Mannlicher rifles and two hundred Schwarzlose machine guns. A Vienna newspaper broke the story of the illicit diversion and the weapons were confiscated, but the Hirtenberger arms scandal helped inflame relations between the Left and the Right at a time when the Austrian chancellor, Engelbert Dollfuss, had suspended parliament, invoked emergency rule, and outlawed the Socialist Party. "The *Heimwehr* and its principals, Starhemberg and Mandl," a historian writes, "earned the undying hatred of the Austrian and international Left for their bloody role in the suppression of Vienna's Socialists in February 1934." Ostensibly (and cynically) searching for clandestine Socialist weapons caches, the *Heimwehr* provoked the Socialists into defending themselves in a series of bloody clashes centered on Vienna that resulted in more than a thousand casualties, including several hundred deaths.

After that brief civil war, Nazi sympathizers in Austria increased their agitation for a merger of Austria with Germany. Dollfuss turned to Mussolini for support. "Austria may be assured she can count on Italy at all times," the Italian dictator responded in a speech on 18 March. "Italy will spare no effort to assist her." Dollfuss pushed through a new, dictatorial Austrian constitution styled on the Italian Fascist model, which took effect at the beginning of May. As a reward for the backing of Starhemberg's *Heimwehr*, Dollfuss appointed the young prince as his vice-chancellor, and when Austrian Nazis assassinated Dollfuss in an attempted putsch on 25 July 1934, Starhemberg briefly became Austrian head of state. Mussolini rewarded Mandl the following year, and indirectly funded the *Heimwehr*, by assigning the lucrative munitions contract for his Ethiopian campaign to Hirtenberger.

"Mandl also sold arms to Bolivia during the Chaco War," the historian writes—a brutal war fought from 1932 to 1935 between Bolivia and Paraguay—and reportedly armed both sides in the Spanish Civil War that began in July 1936. And despite his support of the Austrian nationalist *Heimwehr*, Mandl sold munitions and munitions development services to Nazi Germany during these years as well.

Mandl revealed at least some of his business activities to his wife. "He would often ask my advice about matters of importance," Hedy recalled. "I think he asked me not only because he had, though he would not ever admit it, a respect for my judgment, but also because he knew that I was never afraid to tell him the truth. And a man in his position cannot often be sure that people will tell him the truth."

He was not always happy with Hedy's response, however:

Sometimes he would get flaming angry at me for speaking the truth to him. Once we had one of our most terrible battles because I told him that I couldn't *bear* his power—I couldn't bear it that he could buy everyone and everything. I told him that there

were things he couldn't buy, had he ever thought of
that . . . that there are things no one can buy, devotion
and loyalty and love—yes, and *love*, I said. And some
day, I warned him, he would find this out and on that
day he would be lonely and without friends. He was in
a rage with me. But just the same he always came back
to me for my opinion.

Hedy's opinion of business matters was evidently the only
opinion Mandl welcomed from his wife. "Soon I knew that
as in my own house I had nothing to say, so in my own life
I had nothing to say either. And as I, too, am an autocrat,
disaster was inevitable." The dining room of the Mandls'
house was hung with Gobelin tapestries, the windows glazed
with antique stained glass. The "huge, long table" that ran
down the center of the room seated twenty-four, and Mandl
had bought himself what he called "a nice Christmas present"
one year of a solid-gold table service. Hedy remembered the
long table covered thick one dinner-party evening with blue
violets, "and in these blue violets were scattered lots and lots
of orchids so that it was all a deep rich blue and with those
golden dishes, it looked but *fantastic*."

In the midst of such lavish abundance, Hedy said, "we
entertained and were entertained by diplomats and men
of high political position, makers and breakers of dynas-
ties, financiers who manipulate the stock exchanges of the
world." Mussolini was a guest, Austrian and German gener-

als and admirals, but not Hitler: the Nazis classified Mandl as a Jew—"the Jew, Mandl," Joseph Goebbels would call him contemptuously in a 1937 speech. Hedy was reduced to a graceful automaton by the protocol of such events, by her husband's expectations of her, and by her own indifference as well. "I did not do more than smile when I should smile and look grave when I should look grave. I was not interested enough in these things to play an active part in them."

She was not deaf, however. She listened to what was said. She was far more intelligent than her husband and his guests gave her credit for. "Any girl can be glamorous," she would famously say. "All you have to do is stand still and look stupid." She did, but she listened and learned.

She and her powerful husband were not always unhappy. "There were times when we had fun together," she said. "There were times when we were good friends. . . . There were times when we went on hunting trips together, the two of us alone. We would sit for long hours concealed behind a camouflage waiting for our quarry. There were long hours of solitude and silence which, I think, we shared happily."

But Mandl was an insecure and jealous man. He assigned someone among their servants to listen in to Hedy's phone calls. If she spoke the word "picture," he was livid, even if she only happened to be discussing something to hang on the wall. "He was always afraid that I would try to go back to the stage," she said, "back to pictures. At such times he would always taunt me with *Ecstasy*, hurl reproaches and cruelties at me." When they dined out, he brooded in constant surveillance. "My husband would sit there smoking and watching me, watching me and not speaking at all except to say now and then, 'Who are you looking at? Who is there at that table where you are looking?' Things like that. At first I tried always to explain, to laugh at him for being so foolish about nothing. But then, after a time, I did not try to explain at all. It was useless."

Early in 1935, everything changed for Hedy. She had already made two attempts to escape, she would claim, "but both times I was caught and brought back. And I was watched and guarded more closely than ever." What changed was her father, the person to whom she had always been closest. "One night we were all at dinner at one of our hunting lodges where we were spending a holiday," she said. "In the middle of dinner my father rose from the table and asked to be excused. His face was white, his eyes were strange, and I felt a sickness at my heart. I felt that something must be wrong with him, very wrong."

The next day Emil Kiesler seemed better. He denied that anything was wrong with him. "But still he did not seem to ever be quite himself again after that night," Hedy said. "He looked tired and he gave up many of the sports at which he had always excelled. He worried me and every day I went to my parents' apartment to see him."

Then one day it was too late:

I was out driving with a woman friend of mine. We drove finally to the apartment house where my parents lived. My mother, I knew, was out. My father was out, too, I thought, it being early in the afternoon, not more than two o'clock. Well, I would wait for a while and then go up. And so we sat in the car and talked, my friend and I. We must have sat there talking for half an hour. . . . At last I happened to glance up at the windows of my parents' apartment. And it was as if some icy hand had caught my heart. I think I knew right then.

"Look," I said, "the shades are all drawn! Why should they have the shades drawn at two o'clock in the afternoon?"

I jumped out of the car as if I were shot and rushed up the stairs. I opened the door of the apartment, realizing that it was strange I did not have to ring or knock or use my key. A strange man met me in the hall. I saw other strangers there, one or two neighbors standing about. . . . The strange man said to me, "Are you the daughter?" I said that I was. And then he told me that my father had passed away *twenty minutes ago*.

So while I had been sitting outside in that car, while I had been talking of little nothings, while I had been so near him, my father was dying, alone.

Emil Kiesler died of a massive heart attack. An attack of angina with its severe pain had driven him from the dinner table when Hedy had first realized that he was ill. In the family apartment, after his body was removed, she found a cigarette box on which he had scrawled—"in his last agony," she thought—"Please, Hedy, take good care of Mother."

She grieved for a year. "I wore black, nothing but black. I couldn't face any colors. I couldn't see a mirror. I couldn't face people. Wherever I went I could see my father as I had seen him last. And during all this time—I must say this—my husband was very kind to me, very helpful to us all." After a year she recognized that it was time to cease grieving. "It was not fair to my mother. . . . It was not fair to my father. He would have disliked such grief."

Great trauma is always transformative. Identity shatters and with luck a new identity forms. Hedy had changed, as she knew. "From the moment of his death I was completely changed," she said. She had tolerated a bad marriage while her father was alive. "Now I knew that I must run away, must escape, must make my plans to go to Hollywood. I had met death for the first time and death had shown me, among other things, how brief life is. I must have my life, the only life I ever really wanted, before it ran away from me into the dark."

Escape would not be easy. It would take time and planning. It might even take blackmail. She could blackmail Mandl into letting her go if she acquired business secrets he would fear to see revealed. She would have to be a sponge when the German admirals and generals came to dine with them. All she had to do was look glamorous and listen. That was all Fritz expected of her anyway.

By autumn 1933, George and Boski Antheil had settled into an apartment on the top floor of a brownstone at 51 East Fifty-fifth Street in Manhattan. Antheil's opera *Helen Retires* was well along in rehearsals at the Juilliard School of Music. It was based on the 1925 novel *The Private Life of Helen of Troy* by the novelist, pianist, composer, Columbia University humanities professor, and Juilliard president John Erskine, who also wrote the libretto for the opera. (In 1927, Alexander Korda had directed a silent film based on the novel as well, with his actress wife, María, playing Helen.)

"Things were pretty tough," Boski recalled of this period in their lives. "Emotionally and financially. George had been away from America for a long time, and was almost considered as a European composer, so it was difficult for him to get into the swim of American life. His works were not played, for the *Ballet mécanique* was still remembered. . . . And it was, as usual, in spite of no money, an interesting and stimulating life." Their apartment had three "enormous" rooms, Boski said, all leading off individually from a main hallway. The rent was low, but they decided to sublet the third room anyway to share the cost. For recreation, besides music and the parties they held with wine or punch to help the conversation flow, there was always the spectacle of the city:

> We also had the roof to ourselves and spent many hot evenings there, and George again assembled his telescope. . . . And although we did look at the stars often

enough, we used the terrestrial lens and had interesting views of the skyscraper apartments. I always think it is so funny when people live in one of the high stories of such an apartment, they never think that anyone can look at them. Although we did not see anything spectacular, it was interesting to watch people eat, work, argue, without hearing what the words were.

Antheil had the pleasure of reuniting with his family again; his younger brother Henry was clamoring to follow in his footsteps to Europe:

We are around our family dining table over the shoe store on Broad Street. Henry, my brother, is there . . . and dreaming of going abroad—the wanderlust is strong in all of us. Justine, my sister, is there; she is young and smaller than Henry, and like most girls is particularly close to her father whom she adores. Dear mother is in the kitchen making wonderful mashed potatoes and bringing in the pot roast. Boski, my wife, and I are there too. Dad sits there, utterly delighted. Henry and I kid one another, and Justine joins in. . . .

Dad, in his quiet way, sits in the middle of this scene, and dominates it. He considers Boski as another daughter, loves her as his own. These are his children. He looks very happy. There are many such days, week upon week.

Henry, born in 1912, enrolled at Rutgers University in 1931 after graduating from high school. He had continued to urge his older brother to help him travel abroad, and when George returned to the United States in 1933, he put Henry in touch with Bill Bullitt. The Antheils' wealthy friend from Paris had returned to politics and government with the election of Franklin Roosevelt; the president had just appointed him to be the first U.S. ambassador to the Soviet Union. "Bill told me to send Henry down immediately," George recalled. "Henry went and talked Bill into taking him with him to Russia, although Henry had not yet finished whatever kind of diplomat's course he was taking at Rutgers."

Bullitt, Henry and "a whole coterie of young people" left for the Soviet Union in February 1934—"before the premiere of *Helen Retires*" at Juilliard on 28 February, Antheil writes, "which was probably just as well. *Helen Retires* flopped."

The failure of his opera, following upon the earlier American failure of *Ballet mécanique*, battered Antheil to a compositional standstill. "Bewildered," he wrote, "I stopped composing for a time . . . to think things over." The hiatus would last six years. Later he would call this period of inactivity both "a great plus and a great minus. It was a *great plus* in that it permitted me to study, for five or six years, with no other idea in mind except to learn everything about the music of the past that I could. During this time, for instance, I analyzed every great symphony or great chamber work available; and this analysis was not a schoolboy one, but made in great detail and with painstaking care." It was a great minus because "no compositions of mine were played before the American or international public. I refused to allow those already written to be played; I also refused (until I was ready) to write new ones."

Whether or not he was willing to work toward new art, he still had to make a living. George Balanchine, one of the few who had actually liked *Helen Retires*, commissioned him to write a ballet—as it turned out, the first of several for the Russian choreographer. It was supposed to be "American," Antheil writes, and it would be, but the dances that Balanchine's American Ballet troupe presented were "pure Paris à la Russe." Antheil was hungry enough, and therefore flexible enough, to write in the style Balanchine wanted, which Antheil calls "an American ballet *sufficiently Parisian!*" He also composed two dance ballets for Martha Graham in 1934 and 1935.

Another opportunity emerged when a successful team of theater and film writers, Ben Hecht and Charles MacArthur, came east from Hollywood to Paramount Studios in Astoria, New York, across the East River from Manhattan, with enough funding to make six films. When their music director, Oscar Levant, quit, early in the project, they engaged Antheil to score the first of the six. "I had to accept this offer," Antheil explained warily to Mrs. Bok, "not because of the money, which actually is very very little considering the enormous amount of work entailed, but because if my music to this film is successful, it will be a way of earning a living, possibly the only way that a composer can make a living in the United States; certainly it is absolutely impossible any other way."

Hecht remembered a more beneficent collaboration. "MacArthur and I lured Antheil into making money by writing music for movies," he recalled. They shot the first film in the series, *Once in a Blue Moon*, "in the woodlands adjoining the elegant town of Tuxedo, New York." Since the picture was "100% music," Antheil wrote to Mrs. Bok, the story of a clown "which has as its background Russia," George was needed on the set during filming; he and Boski lived on location that summer of 1934 with the cast and crew "in a 'Russian' village reproduced exactly from some original in Russia by our expert movie-set men." It felt like a paid vacation, Antheil wrote later, and "one of the nicest" he'd had.

"With us," Hecht recalled, "were gypsy dancers and fiddlers, Russian clowns and aristocrat refugees, famous wrestlers and pugilists, lady vocalists, swimmers, fortune-tellers, and a gallery of admiring debutantes" from the wealthy enclave of Tuxedo Park nearby. The picture would be a flop—too many nearly unintelligible foreign accents in the cast, Hecht suspected—but he thought Antheil's music "was delightful. I have never heard a merrier collection of waltzes, polkas, and background tunes than came out of its sound track. George wrote melodies as if he had never heard or written a note of modern music." Even one of the animal characters had its theme. "There was a sway-backed old horse named Bombonetti in the picture. What tunes Antheil wrote for this decrepit nag, Bombonetti! With belly sagging and head hanging, our weary Bombonetti seemed to be dreaming always of spring days and of nymph horses neighing in the glades."

There was hell to pay with Mrs. Bok when summer ended. Evidently, she was no fan of movie music. In September, back in Manhattan, Antheil wrote to her to report all the work he was accomplishing and to put his turn toward Hollywood in the best possible light:

> This summer has been very fruitful, and I have worked hard, and there is quite a lot of new manuscript and new situations and new opportunities. . . . I began working upon my symphony, a new one which I had hoped to enter for the Paderewski Prize, ending upon the 1st of October. I finished considerable of the new symphony when a new situation arose. Ben Hecht and Charles MacArthur, authors of movies like "Viva Villa" and "Twentieth Century" and a host of other successes . . . gave me the job of writing the entire music to [their] first picture. . . .
>
> This, however, prevented me from finishing my symphony, and also lost me the opportunity to write a ballet for Ruth Page and Harald Kreutzberg. . . . However, [Page and Kreutzberg] wished only to pay me $200 for this enormous score, and a whole summer's work.

Nevertheless, Antheil went on for pages, "I really think that I deserve my salt as a young idealistic struggling earnest American composer." He had "more performances this season than any other of my colleagues. Still they are subsidized and I am not." It was "not so much the [lack of] leisure, but also the nervous tension. One comes back to one's native land and sees that one has been abandoned." He hated to ask her, who had been so good a friend, "but the time has arrived when I must either turn to Hollywood and its great organization, and become a part of its mill . . . or be a subsidized symphonic and operatic composer because I am part of that great hope of America for a music of its own":

> If you, who are the only farseeing person in America, as far as I am concerned, abandon us, what shall we do? We can only do what we must do in a country unsympathetic to creative musical art, however sympathetic it might be to REcreative musical art. We must accept the verdict and turn to the beerhall Hollywood robber barons, and be a part of their marauding outfit.

Three days later he wrote to her again asking her to provide him with a monthly subsidy so that he could devote himself entirely to his music. That, finally, was enough for Mary Louise Curtis Bok. She replied apocalyptically on 28 September 1934:

My dear George:

*. . . I must say [your letter] is no different than letters
I have received from you over a long period of years, and
while I am sorry to put any further discouragements in your
path, I do not feel inclined to do what you ask and provide
you with a monthly stipend. To do so would imply an interest in your work that I really do not have. . . .*

*I have watched the quality of your work—not always,
it is true, through my own eyes, but I have kept tabs on it
through various people in the musical world whose judgment
I trust. Not once have they reported favorably to me of your
output.*

*I know all your arguments as to lack of success, and quite
evidently you place the blame anywhere but on yourself.
Your egoism has displeased me, for it transcends a rational
self-confidence. The successes you quote in your letters to me
have never had the endorsement of those whose judgment I
trust. . . .*

*That I have advanced sums the past years has been
simply from humanitarian reasons, knowing how badly
up against it you and your wife were. If I do not at last
speak out and tell you this you will continue to be misled,
interpreting my assistance as my faith in your musical gift,
which faith has, alas, become nil.*

*Now, my dear George, you know how I feel about it, and
I think you must make up your mind to stand on your own
feet and make your own living.*

He was wounded, of course, deeply wounded. His response, pointedly written on Hecht-MacArthur Astoria studio stationery, was by turns confidently assertive, respectful or mock-respectful, and grandiose. He was wounded that she thought him conceited; how little she would ever realize the courage it took to write her those letters throughout the years "wherein I *had* to represent myself in my best light . . . or better!" Music was "a strange and beautiful thing," and it would not be made by the opinions of "conservatory professors, however excellent, or by the opinions of antiquated once-great artists out of sympathy with the radical creations of the newer generations." Neither would it be made by "the critics, nor by the orchestral conductors." Yet she had been "more than generous. God bless you." He thanked her from the bottom of his heart. "Goodbye," he concluded. "I shall show you someday that your friends have been wrong. But never again in writing. I am afraid that this shall be my last letter to you, Mary Louise, whom I have *not* betrayed." He signed it: "Faithfully—George Antheil."

But of course it was not nearly his last letter to his reluctant patron. He would continue to write to her for six more years, and continue to ask for support, or for investment in one or another of his ventures. In the meantime, he had to find a way to feed and house himself and Boski. Movie music would be one solution.

Writing might be another. In *Bad Boy of Music*, as he did with so many of his struggles, Antheil makes a lighthearted story of his pursuit in 1935 of a writing commission from Arnold Gingrich, the editor of the two-year-old men's magazine *Esquire*. George, Boski, their costume-designer tenant, Irene Sharaff, and their sometime post-performance visitor George Balanchine would sit up late drinking Boski's good Viennese coffee and gossiping:

> We had been discussing the subject of how most men
> are unwilling to believe their wives or mistresses
> unfaithful and are usually the last to stumble upon that
> fact. We were merrily racing through the lists of our
> acquaintances when, suddenly, the thought occurred
> to me: "Why not write this up for *Esquire*?"
> I did so immediately, twenty-five little squibs, each
> one an instance of how to detect unfaithfulness. I
> labeled them, "She Is No Longer Faithful IF," and
> sent them off to Arnold Gingrich, *Esquire*'s editor.

Gingrich knew a good feature when he saw one. *Esquire* was based at the time in Chicago; he set up a breakfast appointment with Antheil for the following week, when he expected to be in New York. Over breakfast at the Plaza hotel he offered the composer $250 per batch of twenty-five squibs if he would produce sixteen batches.

Antheil did the math. He was stunned. Sixteen batches times $250 was—"FOUR THOUSAND DOLLARS! [About $65,000 today.] Holy smoke!"

If he could sell this editor his late-night musings, Antheil thought, maybe he could sell him his hobbyist venture into endocrinology as well. Antheil had been an amateur student of endocrinology for years, ever since a roommate in Berlin had left behind an endocrinology textbook when he moved out. Voracious reader that he was, Antheil had devoured it and become fascinated with what he took to be the possibility of predicting behavior according to which hormones appeared to dominate a subject's physiology. "By the way, Mr. Gingrich," he now spoke up, "would you also be interested in a series of articles on how to recognize which girls will and which girls won't? I have worked out a very scientific method, via endocrinology."

Gingrich was skeptical. He asked for a demonstration. Antheil, nothing if not bold, "analyzed the next fifty girls that came down the Plaza staircase." Gingrich happened to know one of them. Evidently, the composer called her correctly. "I went home that morning with exactly five thousand six hundred dollars' worth of ordered articles," Antheil concludes. Gingrich had even offered to pay in advance.

FIVE

Leaving Fritz

Hedy never specified in detail which German technological advances she heard discussed over luncheons and dinners in the Mandl mansions, but there was much to hear. In 1935, the monocoque-bodied Messerschmitt Bf 109 fighter and the dual-use Heinkel He 111 bomber both saw their first flight tests. The small, heavily armed cruisers that the British called pocket battleships began entering service in the German navy. In 1936, the first of the new Type VII diesel-electric attack submarines was commissioned, and Adolf Hitler began planning his *Westwall* of defensive fortifications opposite France's Maginot Line.

Certainly Hedy listened closely to discussions of submarine and aerial torpedoes, weapon systems for which Hirtenberger was supplying components. The genius of German torpedo development at that time was a northern German mechanical engineer named Hellmuth Walter. Born with the century and educated at the Hamburg Technical Institute, Walter was particularly interested in submarine propulsion, which was limited by the problem of supplying oxygen underwater to sustain combustion.

The standard submarine of the day (and throughout World War II) used diesel engines for surface operation, where it could draw in air from outside the vessel. Underwater, with no available air supply, it had to switch to battery-powered electric motors, which limited its speed and the time it could remain submerged before its batteries had to be recharged. On the surface such a submarine might make 17 knots ("knots" is a phonetic abbreviation of "nautical miles per hour"; 1 knot equals 1.15 miles per hour). Underwater it could make half that speed at best, while the ships it might be stalking could pull away (or hunt it down) at surface speeds of up to 35 knots. Walter wanted to find a means, he wrote, "to drive a submarine at much higher speeds than the conventional 6 or 8 knots, submerged."

In the 1920s, while employed as a marine engineer at Stettiner Maschinenbau AG Vulcan in Stettin, on the Baltic, Walter worked out his ideas: Instead of carrying fuel for engines that needed air to sustain combustion, preventing their operation underwater, why not identify an oxygen-rich fuel that could be chemically decomposed to supply its own oxygen, and use that reaction to drive a turbine directly? There were such fuels. Pure oxygen was obviously one, but storage in a small space such as a submarine would require that it be cooled to a liquid and maintained there, below its boiling point of -297.33°F. Nitric acid was another, with 63.5 percent oxygen available when decomposed, but it was highly corrosive and difficult to store and handle.

A little research led Walter to hydrogen peroxide, H_2O_2, a liquid slightly denser than water first isolated by the French chemist Louis Jacques Thénard in 1818. Used in low concentrations, up to 30 percent, as a bleaching agent and a disinfectant, hydrogen peroxide at high concentrations could be decomposed by contact with an appropriate catalyst into steam and oxygen—$H_2O + O$—in the process generating intense heat: 80 percent H_2O_2 when it decomposed would generate a temperature of 869°F, superheating the steam sufficiently to drive a power plant without adding any additional fuel. Fuel could be added, however, drawing on the oxygen released from the H_2O_2 for combustion and further superheating the steam, increasing its propulsive energy. In the first case, the purity of the H_2O_2 would determine the rate of energy release; in the second, the injection of a fuel such as alcohol or kerosene into a combustion chamber to mix with the decomposing H_2O_2 could be throttled to vary the output on demand. In either case, the energy would be generated without the need for additional air.

Walter found very little available research on the use of hydrogen peroxide for energy production, he recalled, "only isolated suggestions which have never been developed beyond the stage of theoretical discussion." Nor was there much interest at Vulcan in H_2O_2 research. Frustrated, Walter took his ideas to the German naval command in Berlin. "Years later," a biographer writes, "colleagues remembered him carrying around papers for his Unterwasser Schnellboot [underwater fast boat], so that he could lobby for his proposals at any opportunity."

The naval command was interested, but before Walter could proceed with research and development, he had to prove to its officials that H_2O_2 was safe for transportation and storage. Higher concentrations were commonly believed to be dangerously explosive, a prejudice that had seriously retarded research. Tests at the Chemical State Institute in Berlin—exploding lead azide, a strong detonator, with H_2O_2, decomposing it under pressure—established its non-detonability up to 80 percent strength. "After the encouraging results of this period of predevelopment and research," Walter writes, "I founded my own engineering firm on July 1, 1935. The real development of engines and rockets started after this date."

From his new Walterwerke (Walter Works) in Kiel, Walter proposed to the German naval command a two-thousand-horsepower hydrogen-peroxide-driven four-man mini-sub designed for underwater speeds of up to thirty knots. With support from Captain Karl Dönitz, already an influential submarine flotilla commander, naval command encouraged Walter's project, which would be awarded a construction contract in 1939. By late 1936, Walter had achieved one thousand kilograms of thrust in a hydrogen-peroxide-fueled turbine. A four-thousand-horsepower system followed not long after.

While exploring development of his new submarine, a potentially devastating weapon, Walter also describes working on missile engines and assisted-takeoff devices (ATOs, temporarily adding thrust, enable aircraft to take off from shorter runways or boost heavily loaded aircraft into the air) for the German air force, the Luftwaffe:

> The first flight with a liquid propellant took place in
> February 1937, with 100-kg thrust. Later in that year
> and during 1938, a great number of flight tests were
> made with ATO's at 300 to 500-kg thrust with land
> and sea planes. . . . All of these were mono-fuel devices
> working with 80 percent hydrogen peroxide. A number
> of unguided missiles were tested, among them a midget
> prototype of the V-2 [rocket] which climbed up to
> 18-kilometer height and broke through the sound bar-
> rier. Rocket-propelled depth charges were thrown over
> 200-meter distances, and sea mines, dropped from an
> airplane, were decelerated so that they fell gently into
> the sea. During the summer of 1939, the first airplane
> took off (Heinkel 178) propelled solely by a control-
> lable rocket. The first torpedoes were launched just at
> the outbreak of the war. In this case, the propulsion
> engine was used with a dual fuel system [of] kerosene
> and hydrogen peroxide.

In addition, and most relevant to Hedy's eventual purposes, Walter and his staff were involved with developing methods of remote control for their torpedoes. They would also have been aware of work at the German Aviation Research Institute in Berlin Adlershof on radio-controlled anti-ship glide bombs, because at least one of the glide bombs under development, the Henschel Hs 293A, used hydrogen peroxide for propulsion.

The German navy's work on torpedo control had begun in 1935, early enough for Hedy to have heard about it. Radio control of submarine torpedoes was difficult—radio signals don't travel far through seawater—and most German specialists favored wire guidance, the torpedo paying out a thin insulated wire behind it as it left the submarine that connected it electrically to a human controller guiding its path. But the anti-ship glide bombs under development for delivery by plane were radio controlled. Furthermore, they used a system of frequency selection that might have offered Hedy one piece of the puzzle of how to prevent a radio-control signal from being jammed.

The radio-control system that the Germans used on their Fritz X and Henschel Hs 293 glide bombs, an American guided-missile expert writes, featured a transmitter that "could operate on any of 18 pre-launch selectable frequencies, spaced 100 KHz apart, between 48 and 50 MHz. This capability was designed into the system to enable coordinated simultaneous mass attacks by formations of bombers and allowed up to 18 missiles to be separately controlled at one time. It also helped to negate the effects of any enemy electronic jamming directed at the guidance system."

So the German system did not move the transmission around among radio frequencies to avoid a jamming signal; it merely assigned the communications between each bomber and its single glide bomb to one of eighteen different radio frequencies, allowing each plane to control its own bomb without radio interference from other bombers, which had similarly been assigned different exclusive frequencies spaced one hundred kilohertz apart in the frequency band between forty-eight and fifty megahertz. Since each bomber-missile pair communicated on only one frequency, the enemy could still jam the signal, but he might need a few minutes to figure out which of eighteen different frequencies he had to jam to confuse a particular bomb heading his way.

Hedy Kiesler Mandl met Hellmuth Walter in December 1936. The occasion was the annual Christmas gala at the Hirtenberger factory in Hirtenberg, Austria. "He was very interesting," she told an interviewer late in life of her meeting with Walter. "As we had dinner, he was talking about his remote-controlled, wakeless torpedo." The torpedo in question was wire guided and hydrogen peroxide powered; the steam that drove the torpedo that resulted from H_2O_2 decomposition quickly dissipated in seawater, leaving no telltale wake, another advantage of the system. The torpedo had other problems, it seemed, related to the relatively small volume of fuel it could carry.

All this knowledge of developing German military technology was Hedy's capital as she prepared herself to leave Fritz Mandl and Austria and find her way to Hollywood. She spoke of it later as protective, as information she could use or did use to persuade Mandl to allow her to leave him, but wasn't it just as likely to be dangerous for her to know? Or did she count on the chauvinism of the German military men with whom she socialized—standing still and looking stupid—to protect her?

Hedy told various tales of how she freed herself from Fritz Mandl. She would have had reason to lie about their breakup. She had already been stigmatized for her appearance in *Ecstasy*—the film had been publicly censored in the United States. Divorce was a scandal in 1930s America; elaborating a story of brutal confinement and clever escape might avoid further stigma.

In the most elaborate version Hedy told, she picked out one of her housemaids who closely resembled her in height, weight, and coloring, befriended the maid, studied the maid's manner until she was confident she could imitate it, drugged her one day by putting sleeping pills in her coffee, dressed in her uniform and slipped out of the house, raced for the train to Paris, filed for a French divorce on the sardonic ground of desertion, and raced on to London to put herself beyond Mandl's grasp. The story is so Bluebeardian that it may well have been an invention of the Metro-Goldwyn-Mayer publicity department.

Hedy came closest to telling the truth about her breakup

with Fritz Mandl in a 1938 as-told-to interview. Even there she left out the backstory, which can be at least partly reconstructed from contemporary newspaper reports and later documents.

After attending the Christmas gala at her husband's factory in Hirtenberg, Hedy spent the winter season at St. Moritz, the fashionable Swiss ski resort where the 1928 Winter Olympics had been held. Her husband did not accompany her. His work may have kept him away—he was already busy sequestering assets in Switzerland and investing in Argentina—or he and Hedy may have separated after one of their escalating series of battles. "I felt more and more," she said in 1938, "every day now, every hour, that I must escape *or be strangled to death* by luxury, by a vain attempt to find happiness."

Part of that vain attempt at St. Moritz was apparently a brief affair with the writer Erich Maria Remarque, famous for his World War I novel *All Quiet on the Western Front* and a man like her father, tall, older, handsome, and confident. Remarque spent two months, January and February 1937, vacationing at St. Moritz, his biographer reports, summarizing his experience afterward in a diary entry. "'Went walking to begin with; afterwards mostly sat in the bar,' his diary records. . . . Then follows a selective list of the people he associated with [including the writers Louis Bromfield and Georges Simenon, the Hollywood stars Kay Francis and Eleanor Boardman, and the film directors Leni Riefenstahl and William Wyler]. . . . Casually infiltrated into the list is the single name Hedy, the only person not fully identified or attributed with an explanatory word or two. Remarque's discretion betrays as much as it conceals the degree of intimacy between them."

Remarque's new novel, *Three Comrades*, had begun serialization in *Good Housekeeping* magazine in January and would be published in May. The novelist's previous works had been burned in Germany in the notorious Nazi-sponsored book burning in 1933, however, and Remarque himself was persona non grata there. It's easy to see what he and Hedy had in common—including, as she would make clear in America, contempt for the Nazis.

A key requirement for a successful transformation of personal identity is a mentor or model to guide the novice over the treacherous crevasse that separates the old identity from the new. Given what followed in Hedy's life that crucial year, Remarque probably filled that role for her. He himself had already transitioned successfully from war-weary soldier to best-selling novelist. He had gone into exile from his homeland as well, driven there by the gathering power of fascism.

Whatever happened between the German novelist and the Austrian film star at St. Moritz, Hedy returned to Vienna sometime that late winter or spring determined to renew her career as an actress. Fritz Mandl was equally determined that she should not. He failed to anticipate that Hedy might appeal to his political partner and close friend Prince Ernst Rüdiger Starhemberg. A report in New York's *Sunday News* on 19 September 1937 describes what followed:

Hedi is expected to appear at the Josefstadt Theatre in Clare Boothe's play, "The Women," which is about to be produced in German.

PALLY WITH STARHEMBERG

Although the invitation to play a leading role came from Director Horch, it is common knowledge here that Hedi arranged the request, presumably through Prince Starhemberg, her husband's closest friend.

When Mandl heard about it, he forbade his wife to visit the theatre and even ordered her not to leave the house.

Prince Starhemberg, Austria's iron man, was seen frequently in Hedi's company until her husband was reported to have told him:

"If this keeps up, our friendship ends here."

The headline told the rest of the story: " 'Ecstasy' Star to Quit Rich Mate for Stage."

Hedy and Mandl had filed a mutual divorce action in Vienna, the story reported. They were not expected to wait for a trial, however, "but would go to Riga, Latvia, the Reno of Europe," for a quickie divorce.

Hedy had not even waited for a quickie divorce, however. By the time the story appeared, she had already escaped to London and was on her way to the United States. The role in *The Women* at the Josefstadt may have been a ruse. Or

Hedy may have realized that she could not remain in Austria with its intensifying anti-Semitism and have taken the first opportunity to leave, as so many other Jewish or anti-Nazi actors and directors were doing—among them Max Reinhardt, Fritz Lang, Billy Wilder, Otto Preminger, Anatole Litvak, Marlene Dietrich, Conrad Veidt, Paul Henreid, Peter Lorre, and Walter Slezak. She did not drug her maid, nor did she leave with merely the clothes on her back. She was both smarter and more practical than that:

> I cannot tell even now how I managed to make my escape. I cannot give the names of the one or two who helped me. Such a revelation would not help *them* now. But I am sure that not in any motion picture would an escape scene be more dramatic. It was at night that I began my packing. My husband and I had another bitter quarrel and he had gone off to one of his hunting lodges. And I had known, as somehow we do know these things, *that this was our last quarrel.* I knew that the time had come, that the hour had struck, as they say in novels, that this time I would succeed. . . .
>
> I packed my jewels and such furs and clothes as I could take with me. I think I had about two large trunks and two small ones and three suitcases. I had to take as many of my jewels and furs as I could manage to carry with me because I could not, of course, take much money out of the country with me. Very little money,

indeed. I knew that I was burning all of my bridges behind me. I was leaving my home. I was leaving my mother and my friends. You do not blame me, I am sure. I was leaving security. But so much stronger than anything else was my wish to come to Hollywood that I had no fear and—I did it.

I managed to leave Vienna that night, veiled and incognito and with all the trappings of a melodrama mystery. And I went straight through to London.

In London, whether fortuitously or by design, Hedy met Louis B. Mayer, fifty-three years old that year, the head of MGM Studios and the highest-paid executive in the United States. Mayer had sailed to Europe some weeks earlier to take the waters at Carlsbad, to inspect the new studios north of London in which MGM had recently invested, and to find writers who could turn out original stories for an American market that went to the movies faithfully twice a week or more.

"At a small evening party," Hedy recalled in 1938, "I did meet Mr. Mayer. We talked a little that night and that was all. He did not speak to me about pictures, nor did I talk to him about what I was doing and where I was going. But I knew very well that Mr. Mayer was the one who would, if he could, help me to take the last step on my long journey to Hollywood."

She told a less demure story later, in her ghostwritten book

Ecstasy and Me, which drew on many hours of interviews and dictation. An American agent, she said, Bob Ritchie, called her in her London hotel room and offered to introduce her to Mayer. She didn't know who he was. Ritchie enlightened her. They went to see him. "I saw *Ecstasy,*" he told her, waving an unlit cigar. "Never get away with that stuff in Hollywood. Never. A woman's ass is for her husband, not theatregoers. You're lovely, but I have the family point of view. I don't like what people would think about a girl who flits bare-assed around a screen." And yet, Hedy adds, "he was giving me close-up inspections from every angle." After more discussion, Mayer offered her a minimal contract: six months at $125 a week if she paid her own way to America. Hedy was confident enough to reject the offer and walk out.

At this point the two versions of the story more or less converge. Hedy wanted a contract with MGM, but she wanted better terms. She therefore had to find a way to impress Louis B. Mayer. He and his wife were sailing home on the *Normandie,* the fast, elegant French ocean liner that was at the time the largest ship in the world, 1,028 feet long and 117 feet wide—more than three city blocks long, that is, and half a block wide—with a service speed of twenty-nine knots, decorated beautifully in contemporary Art Deco.

Hedy bought a ticket. When the *Normandie* sailed on 25 September she was aboard with what she had managed to remove from Austria of her worldly goods. And "on board ship as, frankly, I had hoped, we became friendly, Mr. and

Mrs. Mayer and I." Hedy in the meantime, in her words, "became the center of attention for all the young males aboard, and was able to parade them back and forth past Mr. Mayer." That, and several more meetings and discussions, did the trick: Mayer offered her $500 a week—about $8,000 today—on a seven-year contract "with the usual escalators of $250. All predicated on her agreement to cooperate in taking English lessons and also dependent on her agreement to change her name."

In 1938, Hedy said that Margaret Mayer, Louis's wife, invented her stage name, Hedy Lamarr. "We all agreed," Hedy recalled, "that Hedy Kiesler was not good for the theatre marquees. It was not a name that could be readily pronounced. And so one evening at dinner Mrs. Mayer announced to us, 'I have thought of a name for you, Hedy. What about Hedy Lamarr?' And Hedy Lamarr it was—and is."

The Viennese screenwriter Walter Reisch, a recent hire, was also on board the *Normandie* on that late-September voyage. (So were the William Bullitts, whom Hedy did not yet know, the French actress Danielle Darrieux, the English actress Greer Garson, and many other notables.) Reisch's story of Hedy's renaming is earthier than Hedy's and more detailed:

[Mayer] didn't like Kiesler, because that sounded too German to him, and Germany at that time had fallen into deep discredit all over the world; and he couldn't use Mandl because the husband would create difficulties. So they tried to figure out what to do about her name: Every afternoon they held story conferences around the Ping-Pong table on the "A" deck of the *Normandie* with [Mayer's assistants Howard] Strickling, [Benny] Thau, and all the others, trying to decide how to go about introducing the young beauty to the members of the New York press who would infallibly arrive on the boat.

Now earlier, one of Hollywood's most famous motion picture stars, one of the most beautiful girls in Hollywood—well under thirty—had died. Her name was Barbara La Marr. Somehow that name was the property of MGM. Louis B. Mayer, not superstitious at all, picked that name and said, "We are going to replace death with life." And he coined the name Hedy Lamarr. She had no idea that she was getting the name of a dead motion-picture star. When we arrived at Ellis Island, a girl more beautiful than any ever seen in America, by the name of Hedy Lamarr, came down the gangplank: not anybody's daughter, not anybody's sister or relative . . . a star was born.

Barbara La Marr's death was more than simply the tragedy of a beautiful woman dying young. The actress had in fact been a Mayer favorite whom he had touted as "the most beautiful girl in the world." She had been a heroin addict, and she had died of tuberculosis and nephritis at twenty-nine. If Margaret Mayer had indeed introduced Hedy Kiesler to her new name, a name borrowed from a dead actress who had been a favorite of her husband, a well-known philanderer, was she delivering a blessing or a curse?

Hedy accepted the name change. It was almost the last piece of the puzzle of her new identity, a rebranding that marked her transformation from Austrian actress to Hollywood starlet. The rest was up to her. She arrived in Hollywood in October 1937 and began learning English by screening films with her assigned housemate, the Hungarian actress Ilona Massey. George and Boski Antheil had preceded her by a year.

six

Cinemogling

Louis B. Mayer had picked up a job lot of actors and writers in Europe; he had no special role in mind for twenty-two-year-old Hedy Lamarr when he signed her in September 1937. After she arrived in Hollywood in October, Hedy spent the next six months learning English, losing weight, and killing time. "She swam," *Time* noted, "batted tennis balls, expertly played her piano, stole the show at a few beauty-ridden Hollywood parties, to which she was squired at times by Rudy Vallee, Howard Hughes and lately by actor Reginald Gardiner." When, finally, in April 1938, she was loaned out to the independent producer Walter Wanger to star opposite Charles Boyer in *Algiers*, she had dropped from 125 to 110 pounds on her five-foot seven-inch frame. "It was discovered," *Time* added snidely, "that she would require padding to fill out her bust—a deficiency no cinemogler had noted in *Extase*." (*Time* in those days liked to invent portmanteau words—"cinema" plus "ogler" in this case—in the manner of James Joyce.)

Algiers was a remake of a French film, *Pépé le Moko*, about a jewel thief hiding out in the Casbah, the Arab quarter of the North African city of Algiers, who meets the beautiful French visitor Gaby, falls in love with her, and, in doing so, is delivered to ruin by the jealousy of his Algerian mistress, Ines. "The film and especially Hedy Lamarr were a sensation," writes a film historian. "Pepe and Gaby fall in love and learn that they grew up in the same [impoverished] Parisian quarter. He says: 'What did you do before the jewels?' She replies: 'I wanted them.'" Pepe's invitation, "Come with me to zee *Casbah*," though it was only spoken in the film's trailer, entered the American language. Hedy became a full-fledged Hollywood star. The turbans she wore in the film started a new fashion among American women. Other Hollywood actresses, previously blond, dyed their hair black to match hers and, as she did, began parting it in the middle.

Despite Hedy's new fame, after *Algiers* she once again had time on her hands: Mayer was better at declaiming his managerial gifts than at finding good scripts for his new star. Hedy was not an intellectual, and English was her third or fourth language. Beyond magazines, scripts, and the research necessary to prepare for a role, she was not a reader. Man Ray recalled playing chess with her when he lived in Hollywood in the 1940s. She was of course a trained pianist and played at home both alone and with friends. She made the rounds of parties more from necessity than for pleasure: being seen and meeting the cast and crew of Hollywood—studio executives and her fellow actors—were part of her acclimatization. Even newly arrived, still in her early twenties, she spoke warmly of good friends and good conversation. "My favorite thing," she said in 1938, "is to sit in my own house or in the private houses of my friends where we can talk. I don't like people who kid all the time. My ideal evening is to have dinner quietly with friends and then enjoy their stimulating conversation."

One way Hedy occupied her spare time was inventing. Spending evenings at home working on an invention may sound surprising today, especially for a movie star, when so many other activities beckon through the Web. In 1938 the most common intellectually stimulating entertainments available at home were books, card and board games, and musical instruments. Hedy invented as a hobby. "Howard Hughes once lent her a pair of chemists," *Forbes* magazine reports, "to help her develop a bouillon-like cube which, when mixed with water, would create a soft drink similar to Coca-Cola. 'It was a flop,' she says with a laugh." Her daughter, Denise, remembers a tissue-box attachment Hedy invented for disposing of used tissue. Hedy invented to challenge and amuse herself and to bring order to a world she thought chaotic.

George Antheil had also turned to inventing during the 1930s, but his motives were more practical. "My life has been motivated by one steadfast resolve," he told *Esquire* in 1939, "which is *not to starve to death*. This attitude has embarrassed my friends who had better ideals for me, i.e., to live in a garret, write 'great music,' and gradually starve to death. Because from time to time I write either an article or a movie score as well as 'my serious music,' they consider that I am not fulfilling the great faith and trust which they had originally placed in me." *Ballet mécanique* had started out as a movie score, of course, but since the movie in question was itself avant-garde, it had passed muster with Antheil's "friends."

In the autumn of 1935, with an ample advance from Arnold Gingrich, Antheil had begun writing his series "She's No Longer Faithful If——." The series ran in *Esquire* from April through October 1936 under the droll pseudonym Marcel Desage—was Antheil alluding to the Marquis de Sade? The magazine required a pseudonym to avoid revealing how many of the composer's articles it was publishing, sometimes more than one an issue. Under his own name, in April, *Esquire* carried Antheil's first full-length article on endocrinology, "Glands on a Hobby Horse," and in May, after that introduction, his "Glandbook for the Questing Male," subtitled "Reducing a Laboratory Science to a Sidewalk Sport for a Grading of the Passing Females from A to D."

Antheil fell ill in the midst of all this essaying, in December 1935—"very very ill," he told William Bullitt—with the serious asthma and bronchitis that plagued him during wet winters in those days before antibiotics. He spent January and February largely in bed and told Mrs. Bok later that he "almost died." He and Boski had been thinking of moving to California for his health. He had also become aware of the increasing opportunities in Hollywood for composers, a change that he explained to his peers in an article in *Modern Music*:

> Ten years ago existing musical scores were not protected by copyright from [movie exploitation]. The only expense producers incurred was the cost of having able copyists go to the music libraries or buy sheet music. The contents were available to them without royalty costs. . . .
>
> But now that copyright has been recognized as protecting composers against the sound-film, it costs the movies big money to quote twelve bars from anything or anybody—an average of $100 a measure. Think of a hundred thousand measures, and you will have some idea of the cost of a quoted score, and you will also understand the sudden new vogue for "originals."

These several convergences gave him, he said, "just enough of a taste for motion picture scoring to come out to Hollywood." In 1936 he and Boski bought a car, packed up, and took their time driving out west by way of Charleston, Clearwater, New Orleans, El Paso, and Santa Fe. They lingered in Santa Fe through the summer, collecting friends, until an uncharacteristic spell of July rain shrouded the high desert country, when they proceeded on to Hollywood. "I have made my first great trip across America," Antheil wrote to his patron grandly after he arrived on 1 August. "I have been down to the border of Mexico, and up in Santa Fe. My health seems to have been improved by the westward trip 100%; I really feel fine. I hope, somehow or another, that things might at last go a little better with me—I really feel that I deserve it."

That fall he composed the score for a Cecil B. DeMille film, *The Plainsman*, starring Gary Cooper and Jean Arthur. For a two-hundred-page score he was paid only $750 ($12,000 today), one-third of a three-score contract. He assured Mrs. Bok that established composers earned $5,000 to $7,000 ($80,000 to $111,000) per film. Then Boski announced one day that she was pregnant. The pregnancy was completely unexpected, and the bank account was empty. Antheil asked his reluctant patron to help them until he got out from under his second and third scores, and she did.

The Antheil's only child, Peter, blond and blue eyed like his father, as dark Boski had predicted, was born in June 1937. By then, Gingrich had exhausted his enthusiasm for George's writing, just when George had concluded that he "liked the idea of writing for a living. . . . Writing words, moreover, was not like writing music for the movies; I could write words all day—however corny—and these words would in no manner interfere with my writing music at night." Antheil then "studied the writing field very exactly" and concluded that the most highly paid field of writing was the syndicated column. He undertook to write a "love column" called "Boy Advises Girl" for the new Esquire Syndicate. Within a few months the syndicate was ghosting the column for him—paying him less, he says emphatically, "*but I no longer had to work for it.*" He published a book that year as well, *Every Man His Own Detective: A Study of Glandular Criminology*, capitalizing on and incorporating his *Esquire* endocrinology studies.

He was still living from project to project, however, and with his new sense of responsibility as a father he looked beyond one-off film scoring to invention, which appeared to have the advantage of long-term financial return. Like many novice inventors, he seriously underestimated the difficulty of finding investors. Like other novices as well, he benefited from his ignorance, which liberated his enthusiasm.

In 1924, Antheil recalled, when he was living in Paris, he had conceived "a system of musical notation in which . . . one could write or print music that could be *instantly* read by the veriest tyro." An editor friend of his had suggested he lock in the idea by devising a typewriter that could type the simplified notation and patenting it. He had done so, but the patent had been issued in France, and before he moved to California, he had burned his only copy along with "every last piece of 'valuable paper' which I had previously insisted upon carting around with us all over the world."

He turned to William Bullitt, since October 1936 the U.S. ambassador to France, to help him straighten out the foreign rights and fend off a Dutch challenger who had either independently invented a similar system or stolen Antheil's. At the same time, he reconceived the invention as a scrolling sheet, like a player-piano roll but rolling down vertically, that would guide the novice's fingers to the right keys at the right times to play the music scored on the scroll. (As the sheet scrolled down above the piano keys, vertical black bars printed on the sheet emerged and passed by above the keys to be played. The length of the bar as it passed by dictated how long a key should be held.) He called his invention SEE-Note.

By the time Bullitt reported back on the French patent (expired) and the Dutchman (not a threat but a successful example of how many copies of the SEE-Note system an energetic promoter might sell), Antheil could report in turn to Bullitt, "Our company, you will be glad to know, is now definitely established; our investors made an analysis of the situation, the sales graphs, and a complete report on the amount of pianos in various locales, etc. etc. and decided to start at $225,000 capital. We shall start October 15th."

Antheil then undertook to convince Mrs. Bok to invest in SEE-Note. He wrote to her with his usual enthusiasm, which looked to the uninformed like megalomania, offering her a 49 percent interest in SEE-Note for $49,000 ($770,000 today) and mentioning in the next breath that he had only thirty-five cents to his name and that he, Boski, and "little Peter" would soon be hungry. He also blamed his former patron for having dismissed his original idea back in 1924, which had discouraged him from pursuing it. Mrs. Bok thought he was once again asking her for support and responded angrily.

Antheil apologized in his next letter. He'd found the

money to go on. If Mrs. Bok invested, she could make millions on his invention and endow the Curtis Institute of Music even more lavishly than she already had. (In 1927 she had shored up her original $500,000 gift with one of $12 million, the equivalent of $155 million today—Antheil was aiming high.) They debated back and forth. She consulted a music publisher, who advised her, "The publishers of the world have vast fortunes invested in plates and in printed copies. In order to do a new notation this tremendous capital would have to be wiped out and this is wholly unlikely." Antheil noted that a music publisher, with a vast fortune invested, was not exactly an objective expert. Then he reported that his potential business partners, businessmen with hard heads and good credentials, would only join the SEE-Note enterprise if they could command a 70 percent share. To forestall losing control, he asked Mrs. Bok to loan him $2,000. (In the process, he looked up the total of her gifts to him since 1922: $26,000, or $400,000 today.) That failing, he decided to start small and asked her to join four other friends investing $200 each.

He might have been Abraham pleading for Jehovah to spare Sodom for all the good it did him financially. Mrs. Bok didn't invest in SEE-Note, and the opportunity of a lifetime once again passed George Antheil by. But he had learned about patents, patent lawyers, and patent searches, and also something of the nature of inventing itself.

It did the Antheils little enough good in Hollywood. "We never learned the game," Boski said later. "Everybody thought that George had sold himself down the river in Hollywood, where the sad fact was that we struggled like crazy to try to keep afloat." They were happier, she thought, after they gave up their original plan of making a killing writing movie scores and then getting out:

> We tried to keep up this mirage for about two years, living it up in a very elegant house, with marble floors, two grand pianos, a nurse for Peter, a maid and four bedrooms. . . . After George made his first picture for DeMille, which was very successful, no other scores seemed to come his way. He knew a man, who at the time was one of the top musical comedy producers, and whom he [had known] in his earlier period, who always said how much he admired George's music and promised him a picture in the very near future . . . and we lived on this promise like silly fools. Until we were behind the rent for many months and decided to ask the landlady, who was an extremely nice person, to take our promissory note for the rent we could not pay, and moved into a small Hollywood bungalow, which brought us a lot of happiness, good friends. We had practically no furniture beyond the bare necessities. It was like being back in Paris.

Mrs. Bok, moving to a new, smaller house herself, had discovered several crates in her basement that Antheil had sent her from Paris and forgotten about. She asked him if he

wanted them. He realized they contained the paintings he
had bought from starving artists in his early days in Berlin
and Paris. He had them shipped to the "small Hollywood
bungalow," Boski writes, where she hung them "on the walls.
But these being paintings by Braque, Picasso, Leger and
other famous contemporary artists, most people would not
have known that they were of any value and would have just
noticed that if we were more than four people, one had to sit
on a cushion on the floor."

Some truly desperate financial crisis afflicted the Antheils
in March 1940. George wrote to Mrs. Bok in despair, the more
so since he had assured her early in 1939, when SEE-Note
was bubbling, that he would never ask her for money again.
Generous soul that she was, she came through with twice the
amount George requested. At the same time the chairman of
the music department at Stanford University invited George
to join the faculty, which he did.

"[We] put our meager possessions in storage," Boski
recalled, "and drove to Stanford with Peter [and] our Japanese student [helper] and settled in a nice house on the campus. But the perversity of Hollywood fate is really funny. No
sooner were we settled in Stanford than Ben Hecht wanted
George to write the score for a picture he was doing, and as
George and Ben were good friends and as salary was not too
high at the university and we were in debt, and if one has
waited for three years for an offer, one can hardly refuse it
when it comes along, George decided he can do both and

would commute from Stanford to L.A. when he was not lecturing."

Antheil did, flying down to Hollywood, flying back to Stanford, "just making it on time for his lecture." They couldn't let Stanford know—"Hollywood," Boski said, "was not a respectable word in academic circles."

The Antheils were still living on the Stanford campus in Palo Alto when word came in late June 1940 that George's cherished younger brother Henry had been killed in a plane crash. Henry had remained at the American embassy in Moscow, serving as the clerk in charge of the code room, when Bullitt had moved on to France. In 1939, Henry had requested a transfer from Moscow to the U.S. legation in Finland, where he arrived just in time to experience the 30 November bombing of Helsinki that initiated the brief, brave winter war between little Finland and the Soviet Union. At the resort hotel outside of the capital where the U.S. legation had moved to avoid the bombing, Henry met a young Finnish woman, Greta Lindberg, and the two fell in love. They quickly became engaged.

It was Henry who had been supplying George with information on the burgeoning war that George had used, along with discussions with Bill Bullitt and his own sharp wits, to write a series of spectacular articles for *Esquire* that were in the process of being assembled into a book that George would publish in the fall, *The Shape of the War to Come*. Antheil had predicted to within a week the beginning of the war in Europe with the German invasion of Poland on 1 September 1939; he also predicted the German surprise attack on the Soviet Union in June 1941 and the Japanese entry into the war late the same year. Henry's inside information came from classified State Department cables that he illegally extracted for his older brother's use. Henry also, according to a recent review, "falsified assignment cables in order to remain together with his Finnish fiancée, Greta." No one ever faulted the Antheil boys for timidity.

The Finns were vastly outnumbered—450,000 Soviet troops to 180,000 Finns, 6,500 Soviet tanks to 30 Finnish, 3,800 Soviet aircraft to 130 Finnish—but the Finns, defending their homeland, fought the Soviets to a standstill in December and January; in one battle alone, Russia lost more than 17,500 men, the Finns about 250. Finally, the Soviet Union invaded en masse, no other country was prepared to come to Finland's rescue for fear of inciting a German response, and the Finns unhappily agreed to a peace treaty that required them to cede territory. The poor performance of the Soviet forces—the Soviet army took 400,000 casualties, including 126,000 dead, compared with Finland's loss of 40,000 wounded and 26,600 dead—encouraged Adolf Hitler in his plans to launch Operation Barbarossa, his surprise attack on the Soviet Union, the following June.

Henry and his fiancée had gone off to Tallinn, Estonia, for a holiday on the weekend of 1–2 June 1940, their last days together. They had returned to Helsinki, but Henry had flown to Tallinn again on the morning of 14 June, the first day

of a new Soviet-imposed blockade of Estonia, to pick up diplomatic pouches from the U.S. legations in Tallinn and Riga.
He left Tallinn at two that afternoon on a commercial flight
back to Helsinki. Five minutes after takeoff his plane, *Time*
reported, "mysteriously exploded in mid-air and plunged
into the Gulf of Finland." A telegram to George Antheil from
Cordell Hull, the U.S. secretary of state, reported that "no
hope is held of recovering the remains of the passengers lost,"
offered "profound sympathy," and said that Henry had been
"killed in an airplane accident." By 17 July, however, the *Los
Angeles Times* reported that the Soviets had shot down the
Finnish airliner, probably because it was technically in viola-
tion of the Soviet blockade.

Hedy's shock of war was less personal than Antheil's. She did
not lose a loved one that summer, but she read and heard of
murdered children even as she adopted a baby boy, separated
from and divorced her second husband, and shared with her
friends Janet Gaynor and Gilbert Adrian, the actress and the
costume designer, the birth of their first child.

"You couldn't live with a person, in those days, without
being married," Hedy explained many years later. She had
met Gene Markey, a screenwriter and man-about-town, in
January 1939. In 1937 he had divorced the actress Joan Ben-
nett, with whom he had a daughter. He met the standard of
the kinds of men Hedy fell for: older (forty-three when she
met him), taller (over six feet), and highly polished. A later

wife, Myrna Loy, described Markey as "a brilliant raconteur, a man of unfailing wit and humor [who] could charm the birds off the trees, although birds were never his particular quarry—women were, the richer and more beautiful the better." Four weeks after they met, on Saturday, 4 March 1939, Hedy and Gene were married at the governor's palace in Mexicali after holding an impromptu press conference in San Diego to announce the event. "We decided late Friday evening that we must get married the next day— or miss our chance," Markey had written to the gossip columnist Hedda Hopper, whom he had not had time to alert. "Hedy did not even get a chance to go home to change her clothes." Both busy professionals, they had returned to work immediately after the weekend. They had already bought a house to go home to, on Benedict Canyon Drive in Beverly Hills.

The marriage lasted only sixteen months. The Markeys separated in July 1940; Hedy filed for divorce on 4 September. She told the court that she and her husband had spent only about four evenings alone together in all the months of their marriage. The judge suggested drily that next time she should take more than a month to get to know someone before she married him.

One result of the marriage was an adoption, although Hedy seems to have pursued adopting the baby boy she named James Lamarr Markey largely on her own. Jamesie, as he was known, joined the Markeys in October 1939 and remained with Hedy after they divorced.

Hedy met Gilbert Adrian, the designer who styled himself professionally as simply Adrian, through their work together at MGM. Born Adrian Adolph Greenberg in Naugatuck, Connecticut, in 1903, Adrian had been the chief costume designer at MGM since he joined the studio as a talented twenty-five-year-old in 1928; his designs were so popular with American women that one MGM film, *The Women*, shot in black and white, opened in 1939 with a ten-minute Technicolor parade of Adrian's fashions. He designed the outré costumes for *The Wizard of Oz*, including Dorothy's famous ruby slippers; he was Greta Garbo's favorite and Joan Crawford's. Most accounts of his life describe him as an openly gay man, but whatever his sexuality he married the actress Janet Gaynor in 1939 and remained married to her until his death, and in the summer of 1940 they had a son. Despite her stardom—she had won the first Oscar for Best Actress in 1929—Gaynor had retired from the film industry at the end of 1938; "I really wanted to have another kind of life," she had explained. Adrian's expensive costumes were falling out of style in the last years of the Great Depression; in 1940 he was preparing to transition to a producer of high-fashion clothing lines. Robin Gaynor Adrian was born the same week in mid-July that Hedy filed for divorce from Gene Markey.

The children whose deaths that summer horrified Hedy were London schoolchildren assembled in Liverpool for transport by ship to Canada to protect them from the German strategic bombing of London—the Blitz—that was expected to begin and did begin in early September, seventy-six consecutive nights between September 1940 and May 1941 that took more than forty thousand lives in London and elsewhere in Britain.

Submarine and antisubmarine warfare between the British and the Germans had gradually loosened the rules of engagement agreed upon between the two belligerents in the London Submarine Agreement of 1936. According to Karl Dönitz, the commander of the German submarine force, Germany responded to a series of British violations of the agreement:

> [German] Naval High Command reacted only with
> extreme caution and step by step to the British mea-
> sures . . . which constituted a breach of the London
> Submarine Agreement. Slowly and one by one the
> restrictions on the conduct of U-boat operations were
> removed in a series of orders from Naval High Com-
> mand—beginning with permission to fire upon vessels
> which used their wireless, which sailed without lights
> and which carried guns, followed (as a result of the
> instructions to ram [U-boats] given to British ships)
> by permission to attack all vessels identified as hostile
> and ending with a declaration of sea areas that would
> be regarded as operational zones. These latter were
> at first restricted, but finally, on August 17, 1940, the
> whole of the seas around the British Isles were declared

an operational zone, in which attack without warning would be permissible.

Twelve days later, the first of two ocean liners carrying children, the SS *Volendam*, with 320 children among 606 passengers, sailed from Liverpool into the middle of the Battle of the Atlantic. A substantial part of the 351 British ships torpedoed and sunk by German U-boats by early September already lay on the bottom of the ocean. "On her second day out," writes a historian—31 August 1940—"the *Volendam* was struck by a U-boat's torpedo at a little before midnight, seventy miles off Ireland's Donegal Coast. The ship and her passengers were fortunate; all eighteen lifeboats were deployed successfully, the seas were calm, and there was, according to the ship's captain, 'no panic whatsoever.'" A purser was killed; all 320 children survived.

The next ship carrying children to refuge sailed to a more bitter fate. The SS *City of Benares*, with 406 passengers and crew, including 101 adults and 90 children being evacuated to Canada, part of a nineteen-ship convoy, was torpedoed and sunk on 17 September 1940. The British Wartime Memories Project describes the consequences:

Four days, 600 miles out to sea, the destroyer HMS *Winchelsea* and two sloops, who had been escorting the convoy, departed to meet eastbound Convoy HX71. Despite a standing order to disperse the convoy and let all ships proceed on their own, Rear Admiral Mackin-non delayed the order. Shortly after 10 pm the *City of Benares* was torpedoed by U-boat U-48. The order to abandon *City of Benares* was given but due to rough conditions and twenty-miles-per-hour winds, lowering the boats was difficult and several capsized. Two hundred and forty-five lives were lost either from drowning or exposure. Rescue did not arrive until [2:15] the following afternoon when HMS *Hurricane* arrived on the scene and rescued 105 survivors.

Only 13 of the children survived, 6 of whom spent seven days in a lifeboat before being rescued by HMS *Anthony*.

It was after this second, horrific disaster—seventy-seven children drowned in twenty-mile-per-hour winds in the bitter North Atlantic, killed by people who spoke her native language and whose country had forcibly annexed her native land—that Hedy, in Hollywood between films, with a new baby boy in arms, decided the Allies had to do something about the German submarine menace. She began thinking about how to invent a remote-controlled torpedo to attack submarines just at the time she met George Antheil, who knew quite a lot about how to synchronize player pianos.

SEVEN

Frequency Hopping

"We were good friends of Adrian, the dress designer, and his wife Janet Gaynor," Boski Antheil recalled in her unpublished memoir. "Adrian had a talent to be able to imitate people's voices and mannerisms and had great fun doing impersonations." Bright people tend to find one another wherever they live, including in Hollywood. A decade later, when the anthropologist Hortense Powdermaker studied Hollywood as if it were an island in the South Pacific, she noted "a few homes where intelligent and gifted people, regardless of their financial status, gather for good conversation and fun, not dependent on elaborate food, heavy drinking or ostentatious entertainment." She might have been describing Hedy's epitome of her "ideal evening," or a dinner party at the Adrians.

Boski and Peter traveled east during the third week of August 1940, George Antheil wrote to William Bullitt, "to visit my heartbroken parents in Trenton." His brother's death, he told Bullitt, "has both saddened me and steeled me in the resolution to do whatever I can best do to help my country, the U.S.A.—the country that Henry loved so dearly—to withstand and defeat the evil, predatory powers that are again loose in the world. And I ask for no easy job. . . . I feel I owe the enemy something very particular." That week before the sinking of the *Volendam* and several weeks before the worse disaster of the *City of Benares* was the week when George and Hedy finally met.

With Boski and Peter gone, George was batching it and miserable in a local hotel, the Hollywood-Franklin, working on a movie score. The Adrians invited him to dinner to make up a foursome with Hedy, who had separated from Gene Markey the month before. Two intelligent and articulate people, both temporarily alone, both native German speakers, both former members of the European artistic community, were reasons enough to put them together. In *Bad Boy of Music*, however, Antheil attributes the invitation specifically to his endocrinology work:

One day around this time, late summer 1940, [the Adrians] said to me:
"Hedy Lamarr wants to see you about her glands."
I said, "Uh-huh."
They repeated, "Hedy Lamarr wants to see you."
"It's funny," I said, "but I keep hearing you both say, 'Hedy Lamarr wants to see you.'"
. . . "But she does, she really does!" they insisted.

"You mean," I faltered, "that Hedy Lamarr wants to see . . . *little* me?"

"Yes," they said, "and moreover we're going to arrange it for next week. Now don't protest."

"Who's protesting?" I said, bewildered.

So George Antheil met Hedy Lamarr one evening in late August 1940 at the Adrians' house. His "eyeballs sizzled," she was "undoubtedly . . . the most beautiful woman on earth," she looked even better in person than she did on the screen, and "her breasts were fine too, real postpituitary." In the rush of all this gushing, Antheil the author fails to explain that Hedy wanted to see him not generally about her "glands" but specifically because she was concerned that her breasts were too small. (In her book, *Ecstasy and Me*, she attributes this canard repeatedly to Louis B. Mayer, which was probably true.)

"You are a thymocentric," George told the actress once the subject of breast size was invoked, "of the anterior-pituitary variety, what I call a 'prepit-thymus.'" She responded, "I know it. I've studied your charts in *Esquire*. Now what I want to know is, what shall I do about it? Adrian says you're wonderful." In his memoir George feigned embarrassment. Hedy pressed him: "The thing is, can they be made *bigger*?" Yes, said George, blushing, "much much bigger!"

When Hedy left, Antheil claimed, she wrote her phone number on his windshield with lipstick.

The next day he called her, she invited him to dinner

"high up in her Benedict Canyon retreat," and over dinner, served by a butler, they discussed the use of "various glandular extracts" that would make "an honest gland" of her post-pituitary (the posterior lobe of the pituitary gland). "And so the bosoms stay up," Antheil concluded his presentation. Later that evening:

> We began talking about the war, which, in the late summer of 1940, was looking most extremely black. Hedy said that she did not feel very comfortable, sitting there in Hollywood and making lots of money when things were in such a state. She said that she knew a good deal about new munitions and various secret weapons, some of which she had invented herself, and that she was thinking seriously of quitting M.G.M. and going to Washington, D.C., to offer her services to the newly established Inventors' Council.
>
> "They could just have me around," she explained, "and ask me questions."

Although Antheil describes Hedy as "very, very bright," he succeeds here in making her sound at least scatterbrained. In fairness, he does add that she had been the wife of Fritz Mandl, had "overheard him and his experts discussing new devices, and . . . had retained these ideas in basic form," but then goes on, "in her beautiful beringleted head—while all the time clever Fritz Mandl didn't think she knew A from

Z." Even this explanation doubles back on itself: Did Hedy invent independently or simply borrow the "ideas" she had "retained . . . in basic form"? The misogynistic debate about whether or not Hedy's ideas were original or borrowed continues to this day. Evidently, Fritz Mandl wasn't the only one who, deep down, "didn't think she knew A from Z."

When Hedy suggested that the National Inventors Council, just established in August 1940, could profitably ask her questions, she wasn't implying she was a prodigy who could spontaneously generate inventions out of nowhere; she was referring to the fortuitous espionage she had conducted over the Mandl dinner table listening to Austrian and German experts discuss their weapons projects and problems. In effect, she was proposing that Washington could benefit from debriefing her about the weapons-development work of the Austrian and German engineering establishments. That was one way she believed she could help the Allied war effort.

Another way she thought she could help was by working on inventions of her own. She had several weapons inventions in mind. In *Bad Boy of Music*, Antheil locates her discussion of one such new weapon during that first evening at her house. But Hedy told an interviewer many years later that the impetus for her idea of inventing a remote-controlled torpedo had been the sinking of the *City of Benares* on 17 September, which was still four weeks away when Antheil first met her. Evidently, Antheil, to make a better story, compressed his several early meetings with Hedy into one.

Several years later, drafting a chapter for his memoir, *Bad Boy of Music*, Antheil described the setting for invention he found at Hedy's house:

> Here, then, and at long last must suddenly come the true solution as to why Hedy does not go out upon joyous evening relaxations to which all Hollywood would only too willingly invite her, why her "drawing room," sure enough, is filled both with unreadable books and very useable drawing boards that look as if they are in constant use. Why apparently she has no time for anybody except something ultra mysterious about which no inside Hollywood columnist has dared to even venture a guess. Believe it or not, Hedy Lamarr stays home nights *and invents!* I believe it because I know.

By 12 September 1940, George could report to Boski that he had only the title music of the film score left to write. He was also working on the edited draft of his book about the war, *The Shape of the War to Come*. A writer who was a friend of his had taken the original manuscript in hand, George reported: "Our pal, Ted Mills, turned out to be an angel . . . and has done such an expert rewrite job with the book that I can hardly believe I wrote it. The facts are all mine, however. They [Longmans, Green] are *featuring* it on their fall list." Antheil had worked himself into exhaustion, however, which had resulted in an accident that needed his doctor's attention:

I have been up so many nights and have lost so much sleep that several days ago I was sharpening my pencils with a razor blade and gashed the forefinger of my left hand, which I promptly tourniqueted . . . and took to [Dr.] Lou Eshman who, fortunately, was home. He washed and bandaged it, saw that it was not serious, and since then I have had to play with 4 fingers of the left hand—until it heals which will not be for another week or two. But it shows you how extremely nervous I am.

Boski and Peter must have been away for most of the month of September, which would be consistent with a long trip by train across the United States and back—six days round trip—and with grieving in-laws; Hedy and George began working on Hedy's idea for a remote-controlled torpedo some time after the 17 September *City of Benares* disaster. When Boski returned at the end of the month, Antheil reports in his memoir, she was suspicious of her husband's new friendship with a beautiful movie star. "Boski was so indignant," he writes, "that I had to bring Hedy down to our house just to show Boski what a nice girl Hedy really was." His wife wasn't convinced, Antheil adds, but "as time went by, Boski and Hedy became good friends anyway. They are really very much alike basically; both are Hungarian-Austrian and have many tastes in common."

Left unsaid in Antheil's public version of Boski's reaction to Hedy is a long-standing conflict between the Antheils over

George's evident infidelities. Writing to Boski from his hotel while she was away, George had reported on his behavior: "I have been a very very very VERY good boy—why this time I haven't even had a girl out to lunch, or dinner, to say nothing of anything else. Why I haven't even spoken to a girl—any girl—alone!!!!! Nor have I wanted to, really." But of course he had spoken to a "girl," to Hedy, and had dinner with her as well, although at that point perhaps only with the Adrians chaperoning. The story, in *Bad Boy of Music*, about Hedy writing her phone number on his windshield in lipstick, whether true or not, is certainly intended to invoke a standard device in B movies of signaling the beginning of a sexual liaison, another marker Antheil plants to demonstrate that he was a certified bad boy.

Yet an affair between Hedy and George seems highly unlikely. Even without heels she was three inches taller than he, and all the men in her life were tall. Boski, for obvious reasons, monitored George's behavior closely. Her skeptical initial response to his friendship with Hedy is one example. Another is her response to an offer from Hedy. The two women may have become friends, but later, Antheil writes, "when Hedy moved down into Beverly Hills proper and discovered that the so-called 'play' house in back of her swimming pool was fully equipped and furnished" and invited the Antheils to move in rent free, Boski turned down the offer, even though the Antheils were, as usual, short of funds. Boski had asked Hedy if she went swimming every day. Hedy had said yes, she did, "but nobody else comes, excepting [her fellow MGM star] Ann Sothern." Boski had then inspected the house and found that every window looked out on the pool. The Antheils stayed where they were.

As late as 1945, George still had to reassure his wife about his behavior when they were apart, writing to her:

> By the way, don't take my letters to the "girl friends" seriously. It hardly ever does occur to me—but once in a long while the darkness still momentarily descends, and in a flash of white anger I sometimes still do whip out—but more and more harmlessly. I know you'll understand what I mean.
>
> Here is the *fact*: I've been away for a month, and I haven't even taken a girl out to dinner, let alone anything else. This for me is a record. Especially with everybody in the world at hand. I promise to stay *true*.

"Whip out," in the context of Antheil's anger, seems to mean "lash out." What darkness was he speaking of? He didn't say, but certainly his struggles for recognition, even sometimes for bare existence, could have been enough to set a small, proud man hunting for sexual conquests.

By 30 September Boski had returned to find George and Hedy working on their invention. George wrote to Bullitt that day, shamelessly name-dropping without explaining why he and Hedy were spending time together, and included her autographed photo. "I get around Hollywood a great deal, because, often, I must," Antheil told his influential friend obscurely, "and the other night when I was having dinner with the ultra-beautiful Hedy Lamarr . . . she expressed such fervent admiration for you that—for the jest of the thing for I know it'll make you smile—I made her go to her cabinet, get out her most gorgeous photograph, and sign that admiration upon it. It may amuse you, inasmuch as I notice that TIME Magazine of this week declares that Hedy Lamarr is the American soldier's favorite, Ann Sheridan coming second."

How did an actress and a composer go about inventing a remote-controlled torpedo? What was original about their invention that allowed them to successfully patent it, as they eventually did? Hedy discussed the invention process at length in 1997 in a telephone conversation with a fellow inventor, Carmelo "Nino" Amarena, who is also an electrical engineer expert in the field of digital wireless communications. "We talked like two engineers on a hot project," Amarena told me, "prompting one another to the next subject. I never felt I was talking to a movie star, but to a fellow inventor. When you talk to a sympathetic mind about technology, gender, age, and experience disappear completely, and soon you're one-on-one with the topic at hand." Hedy told Amarena that she thought first of a torpedo that was remote controlled. For that she thought of radio.

Amarena wasn't sure why she thought of radio when the Mandl dinner table discussions had concerned wire guidance, but there is reference in the working patent documents that Hedy's son Anthony provided to me to a particular 1939

Philco console-model radio with a unique new feature: the retail radio market's first wireless remote control, a six-inch cabinetry cube with a dialer on top with ten finger holes, like the dialer on a dial telephone. The holes matched up with a ring of small indentations impressed into the surface of the cube printed with the call letters of the radio stations set up to be dialed. Inserting a finger into the dialer hole corresponding to the station to be dialed, rotating the dialer, and letting it return signaled the radio to change frequency to that of the desired station. There were dial positions for up to eight radio stations, plus a dial position for volume control and another that would turn the radio off. (It had to be turned on by hand.) Philco called its new remote the Mystery Control. It was essentially a one-tube radio that communicated on a fixed frequency with either one of two models of console radios, the less expensive 39-55RX or the more elaborate 39-116RX. Each had a corresponding fixed-frequency accessory receiver inside its cabinet that processed the signals from the remote.

With reference in their working documents to the Philco Mystery Control, Hedy or George must at least have seen the radio somewhere. The 116RX was Philco's top-of-the-line model, with a ten-tube radio and expensive cabinetry; it cost $162.50, which would be about $2,600 today, and only 20,480 were manufactured. It was too expensive for the Antheils. Hedy may have bought one or received one as a gift in 1939, the first year of its manufacture. With a Mystery Control in hand, changing stations on her Philco radio from across the room, she could easily have conceived the idea of using radio to control a torpedo, changing its direction remotely just as she changed radio stations.

But conceiving a new use for an existing invention that is substantially the same as the old is not usually a patentable idea. Nor did Hedy think it so. She took her idea a step further, not to make it patentable merely, but to solve a problem she foresaw of torpedo control by radio: jamming. How she knew that set-frequency radio-control systems were easily jammed, she never said. The Philco radios that used Mystery Control were plagued with interference problems, and jamming is simply deliberate interference. The radios had to be adjusted in apartment buildings and other close quarters to prevent signals sent in one apartment from changing stations on radios in other apartments, much as early fixed-frequency garage-door remote controls sometimes signaled neighbors' garage doors to open that happened to be tuned to the same frequency.

Another possible model for Hedy's thinking was German research ongoing in the 1930s on radio-controlled anti-ship weapons such as glide bombs, research about which she might have heard over the Mandl dinner table. Radio control had already been pioneered before and during World War I. The Serbian-American inventor Nikola Tesla patented a radio-controlled boat, which could of course be loaded with explosives and serve as a torpedo, in 1898; a text on the subject, *Radiodynamics: The Wireless Control of Torpedoes and*

Other Mechanisms, by a U.S. Navy engineer, B. F. Miessner, was published in the United States in 1916.

Miessner examines the problem of jamming but offers no solution comparable to the one Hedy would eventually conceive. The closest he comes is a system that generates high-frequency signals so far above the contemporary range of signaling frequencies that an enemy would be unlikely to detect it, much less jam it. The system had a serious flaw: had it been developed, it would eventually have started a minor arms race, with each side moving to higher frequencies as previous operating frequencies were overrun. Success would depend, that is, on an enemy's temporary ignorance of a frequency selection rather than on an active mechanism that somehow blocked or evaded a jamming attempt.

A glide bomb, as its name implies, is a winged bomb dropped from a plane that can be guided by radio control of its wing surfaces to glide forward and change direction as it falls, maneuvering toward a target even if the target attempts to move itself out of the way. The Japanese kamikaze suicide planes that plagued U.S. Navy ships late in World War II were essentially powered glide bombs, except that the glide bombs developed in Germany were remote controlled so that no human pilot had to be sacrificed to their operation.

Formal German development of glide bombs began in 1938 with the opening of a research program at the German Aviation Research Institute, but discussions of such technology had been ongoing in the German engineering community during the Spanish Civil War (1936–39), when

the Luftwaffe, which participated in that war on the side of
the Spanish Fascists, struggled with the problem of bombing ships that were maneuvering to evade its aircraft. (It
was the Luftwaffe's notorious Condor Legion that bombed
the Basque town of Guernica in April 1937, the subject of
Picasso's famous painting.) And significantly for Hedy's
possible knowledge of early glide-bomb research, one of
the first bombs that Germany developed, the Henschel Hs
293, used a Walter hydrogen-peroxide rocket to increase its
forward motion enough to prevent it from being overtaken
by its control plane, a serious problem with earlier unpow-
ered models. (When the German glide bombs were deployed
operationally, midway through World War II, they caused
great destruction. Their threat was finally abated by bombing
the limited number of airfields specially equipped to launch
them.)

None of these unrelated developments adds up to Hedy's
invention, but they do suggest what some of the possible
components and extrapolations might be that prepared her
for her breakthrough. Nino Amarena, the inventor and engineer, commented on the phenomenon in our discussion of his
1997 interview with Hedy. "More often than not," he told me,
"the inventive process follows a cascade of ideas and thoughts
interconnected from previous concepts that for the most part
lie separate, unconnected and unrelated. It takes a clear state
of mind, which is usually someone thinking 'outside the box,'
to suddenly or serendipitously see the connection between the
unrelated concepts and put it all together to create something

new." In that regard, the process of invention is no different from the creative process in other fields. Scientific discovery proceeds the same way. So do painting and sculpture. So does creative writing. The results are different, because each process operates on different realities and by different rules.

Hedy's original idea is simple to state: if a radio transmitter and receiver are synchronized to change their tuning simultaneously, hopping together randomly from frequency to frequency, then the radio signal passing between them cannot be jammed. Hedy called this idea "hopping of frequencies," a grammatically German translation of the German compound word *Frequenzsprungverfahren*, "frequency-hopping process"—in colloquial English, "frequency hopping."

Hedy's idea, entirely original, is yet clearly related to the eighteen different frequencies of German glide bombs (assuming she knew of this technology) and the eight different station selections on the Philco Mystery Control. In neither of those cases did the frequencies hop, but in both cases they could be selected manually and the selected frequency used to transmit to a synchronized receiver.

Another, and more charming, version of the origin of Hedy's idea of frequency hopping comes from her son Anthony Loder. Hedy and George, like the skilled pianists they were, enjoyed playing the piano together. One way they entertained themselves was by following each other, one of them starting a selection that the other would then recognize and play in duet, an elaborate version of the game Name That Tune. As Loder told a *Forbes* reporter in 1991, "Antheil and my mother were sitting at the piano one day and he was hitting some keys and she was following him, and she said 'Hey, look, we're talking to each other and we're changing all the time.'" Hedy was free to contradict her son's version of the discovery, and her choosing not to do so endorses its authority.

None of these precursors is mutually exclusive as a source of inspiration for Hedy's original idea. All these partial models and many others besides may have been at work down in the creative ferment of Hedy Lamarr's unconscious. Since she never publicly described the sources of her idea, there's no way to know.

She did describe the next step to Amarena, however. "I didn't know how to do it," she told him. "I explained the basics of the idea, and the implementation part came from George." Antheil was always scrupulous in attributing the original creative idea for their invention of frequency hopping to Hedy. In her comment to Amarena she returns the compliment, but in fact she worked alongside the composer to develop the idea's implementation—in the jargon of patenting, to reduce it to practice. Antheil made that clear in *Bad Boy of Music* when he wrote of Hedy "doing me the honor of phoning me daily concerning appointments to invent a radio-directed torpedo" while he was batching it at the Hollywood-Franklin when Boski was away. Hedy made it clear in a 1945 interview with the military service newspaper *Stars and Stripes*, which reported her remembering "that she and Antheil sat down on her living-room rug and were using a silver match box with the matches simulating the wiring of the invented 'thing.'" (The matchbox and matches were more likely simulating a target ship and the successive positions of a radio-controlled torpedo; Hedy and George submitted such a drawing as part of their patent application.)

The most general claim of George and Hedy's invention in their patent application reads as follows:

In a radio communication system comprising a radio transmitter tunable to any one of a plurality of frequencies and a radio receiver tunable to any one of said plurality of frequencies, the method of effecting secret communication between said stations which comprises simultaneously changing the tuning of the transmitter and receiver according to an arbitrary, nonrecurring pattern.

This carefully drafted claim deliberately avoids specifying the mechanism for "simultaneously changing the tuning." It does so to encompass as much territory as possible within the patent's boundaries. Writing a patent broadly is part of the strategy of patent claiming. A system of whistles and tuning forks or a system of flashing lights and light sensors might serve as frequency-hopping systems. Because of the broad language of the claim, all would be covered by Hedy and George's pioneering patent.

An old and classic legal text, *Walker on Patents*, condenses many court decisions into a description of what constitutes a patentable invention:

> An invention is the result of an inventive act; it consists in conceiving an idea and reducing it to practice. An invention is the product of original thought; it is a concept, a thing evolved from the mind. It involves the spontaneous conception or "happy thought" of some idea not previously present in the mind of the inventor; it is the creation of something which did not exist before. Such is the mental part of the inventive act.

But the "mental part" of an invention is not patentable by itself. The new idea needs a physical embodiment. In the jargon of patent law, constructing that embodiment is called reducing to practice:

> An invention is not complete by the mere conception of the idea; there must be something more than vague notions of some mode of application of the idea. Such idea is a mere conjecture; it creates nothing until it is reduced to practice and embodied in tangible form.

There's an obvious tension in inventing between concept and embodiment. The inventor wants a patent framed as broadly as possible, to dominate as many variations of his invention as possible, giving him the right to demand a royalty from the would-be developers of those variations. But he must reduce his new idea to practice by embodying it in a mechanism or a material to qualify for a patent in the first place. A textbook on inventing explains:

> The invention is not the specimen or set of plans that the inventor will have made after he has been working on his invention for a while; it is the idea of which this embodiment is the result. It will do the inventor no particular good to get a patent on the specific embodiment, because another inventor might start with the same idea and work it out in an entirely different form. If the inventor gets a patent with claims that describe just his own particular structure and no others, his patent will dominate just that particular structure, and no others. But some other embodiments of his idea might be as good as or better than his, in which case his patent would not have much value. In order to cover all the possible different embodiments, it is necessary to get protection on the original idea. To determine what the idea is, the inventor and his attorney have to explore and visualize the art in the vicinity of the new invention, to retrace the steps that the inventor followed in his original development, and to get rid of the cogwheels and levers and other mechanical elements, until nothing is left but the idea of a certain means used in a certain way to do a certain thing.

Reduction to practice once meant meeting the U.S. Patent Office requirement that the claimant provide a miniature working model of the invention to demonstrate its operation. The Patent Office dropped that requirement in 1880, allowing instead for what it called "constructive" reduction to practice, meaning "construed" or, as we would say today, "virtual" demonstration—drawings and a written description instead of a physical model. But the model or the drawings and description could be, and usually are, only one example of how the invention might be embodied in a working machine. There might be "cogwheels and levers and other mechanical elements" in the machine the inventor draws or builds to demonstrate how his invention would work in practice; but unless the patent is poorly drafted, the machine designed to demonstrate the new idea would not necessarily be the *only* way the invention might be embodied. The distinction is important. Hedy and George would come into conflict with the service to which they would offer their invention—the U.S. Navy—because the naval officers with whom they dealt failed to understand the distinction between their broad patent and the machinery they devised on paper to demonstrate how it would work.

Hedy had the idea of frequency hopping. She needed George Antheil to help her reduce it to practice. According to him, writing in his draft memoir, she chose him because he had some familiarity with munitions—a certificate preserved among his papers in the Library of Congress shows that Antheil worked for an unspecified period of time as a certified inspector of artillery ammunition at the U.S. armory in Tullytown, Pennsylvania, beginning on 12 August 1918.

It seems that Hedy had discovered that somewhere along the line of my perhaps not too nefarious but certainly varied past I have at one time been a government inspector of U.S. munitions. Albeit my knowledge of the same was at this particular moment a bit dusty, nevertheless I was undoubtedly the only "munition brains" available at that time, and Hedy had decided that I would have to do. Hedy, it seemed, had invented a marvelous kind of new munition which she wanted to perfect with me and offer to the U.S.A. government.

If so, then her choice was fortuitous, because Antheil was also, and more significantly, something of an expert on making machines talk to each other in synchrony. He had tried and failed to synchronize sixteen player pianos in the early performances of his *Ballet mécanique*. He had succeeded in synchronizing four player pianos at his Carnegie Hall concert in 1927. In the fall of 1940, he and Hedy now proceeded to work together to apply that knowledge to the problem of creating a frequency-hopping radio signal and synchronizing its frequency changes between a ship or an airplane and a torpedo.

EIGHT

Flashes of Genius

Hedy's divorce from Gene Markey became final in October 1940, just as George and Boski Antheil were moving into a rental house at 1246 North Sweetzer Avenue, on the flats below the Hollywood Hills. "We are, at this instant, engaged in hanging up some of our pictures," George wrote to William Bullitt on 16 October, "a Leger, several Picassos, several Kubins, a Braque, several Marcoussis, etc. And we have just added several new pieces of furniture made for us by Adrian, the Hollywood designer. Both Boski and Hedy send their best to you. Hedy is a quite nice, but mad, girl who besides being very beautiful indeed spends most of her spare time inventing things—she's just invented a new 'soda pop' which she's patenting—of all things!" The "soda pop" was the cola "bouillon cube" that Howard Hughes was helping Hedy develop that eventually flopped. One price of George's failed SEE-Note project had been selling two of his paintings in a poor market depressed by the war and the crowd of refugees from Europe who were selling their artworks as well.

Hedy and George worked together on their invention in the evenings through the fall and early winter of 1940, embodying Hedy's original idea of frequency hopping in an appropriate mechanism—in patent language, reducing it to practice.

The basic problem of transmitting a frequency-hopping command signal between a ship or an airplane and a torpedo was that of synchronizing the transmitter and the receiver so that they could hop together from frequency to frequency. In the first version of their invention, the one they would offer in outline to the National Inventors Council in December 1940, they described a system that relied on human operators to coordinate the signaling, which the ship launching the torpedo would control.

First the ship would determine the maximum time its torpedo would need to travel from ship to target. Next it would add on a certain additional amount of time to allow for currents and torpedo and target maneuvers. Next the ship would contact the observer plane, and the two would verify the time total and agree on it. They would also agree on the intervals of time into which the ship-to-torpedo communications would be broken down, intervals when both plane and ship would observe radio silence. During those intervals, the torpedo would be running on its own on whatever course had been set for it.

Between those intervals of radio silence, however, in

brief, "split-second" communications, "the plane overhead will flash directional corrections and the launching ship will immediately thereafter flash the correctional radio pattern over its proper wavelength for that particular interval." Bundled into this sentence is the idea of changing frequencies each time another signal is sent to the torpedo—the crucial phrase is "over its proper wavelength for that particular interval"— but the two inventors fail to, or choose not to, specify a mechanism for changing the "wavelength"—the frequency—of the signal. They may have decided not to make their mechanism public, whatever it might be, until they had patented it. Or, more probably, they had simply not yet worked out what the mechanism would be.

The latter possibility seems more likely given the afterthought of the phrase. The archaeology of the creative process reveals itself in these layers, beginning with the first. *Idea One*: radio control of a torpedo to increase its chances of hitting its target, something U.S. torpedoes did not yet have. *Idea Two*: "split-second" radio signals between plane, ship, and torpedo in quick bursts between intervals of radio silence. *Idea Three*: changing the frequency of those split-second signals by some undetermined mechanism, adding another layer of complexity that a would-be jammer would have to puzzle through. The Lamarr-Antheil radio-controlled torpedo had reached this point in its evolution when the two inventors offered their ideas to the U.S. government in December 1940.

It was not their only offering. Hedy and George worked

on at least two other inventions during this period besides
their torpedo. "In the meantime," Antheil wrote early in
1941, "Hedy's finished off no less than three 'secret weapon'
gadgets and sent them off to the National Inventors Council . . . and [we] have in due time received our serial numbers pending the War Department's complete investigation."
The change in the wording of this sentence from singular—
"Hedy's"—to plural—the implied but missing "we" and
"our serial numbers"—indicates that George as well as Hedy
was involved in these other efforts.

One of them, the only one for which information sur-
vives, was an anti-aircraft shell fitted with a proximity fuse.
Hitting a moving target such as an enemy bomber high in
the air was an extremely difficult challenge for ground-based
anti-aircraft crews. Thousands of shells had to be fired to
swarm the area around and ahead of an attacking plane,
and even with such a prodigal expenditure of munitions the
chances of a clean hit were small. The American development
of a radar proximity fuse at the Carnegie Institution of Washington, delivered to the military in 1943, was an achievement
of even greater wartime importance than the development
of the first atomic bombs. A proximity fuse detects a target
and detonates an explosive shell at a predetermined distance
away, turning a near miss into a hit. Accurate aiming is still a
challenge, but far more enemy aircraft were shot down during World War II using radar proximity shells than conventional munitions. Such proximity shells saved thousands of

American sailors from Japanese kamikaze attacks in the last year of the war.

Germany was working on a proximity fuse in the 1930s, raising the possibility that Hedy could have heard about such a device during her Mandl years. In November 1939, information on German secret weapons, including the proximity fuse, was passed to British intelligence by an anti-Nazi German physicist, Hans Ferdinand Mayer, in the famous Oslo Report he wrote out in an Oslo hotel room and sent to the local British embassy. The proximity fuse Mayer described in his report worked not by radar, which was still in a primitive stage of development, but by using the electrical phenomenon known as capacitance to sense the presence of a large conductive body such as an airplane. The fuse as designed was not successful; the German program was frozen in 1940 to give priority to other research and ultimately abandoned.

Germany did develop naval magnetic mines during the war, however, and like the German mines, Hedy and George's proximity shell generated a magnetic field to sense the presence of a large metal body such as an airplane. George undertook to handle submitting the idea to the National Inventors Council in early November 1940, which led to a dispute in January 1941 between him and Hedy that threatened their partnership.

At some point in the fall of 1940 they had introduced Louis Eshman, the doctor who had bandaged George's finger when he cut it with a razor blade sharpening pencils, into their inventors' group as a witness. Witnessing to the stages of development of an invention as they occur is important to establishing priority. (Eshman may have been Hedy's doctor and on loan, as it were, to Antheil when he wounded himself. Certainly the physician's loyalties were to her, not to Antheil.) Having joined the group, Eshman soon began to suspect Antheil of withholding information about Washington's response to the magnetic proximity shell proposal, something a person might do who meant to cut his partners out of a claim. When Hedy accused Antheil of such dereliction, he was understandably incensed.

In the beginning, the composer reminded Hedy in a letter he wrote to her on 10 January 1941, they had agreed to an equal partnership. He had not questioned the arrangement until lately, and he wasn't doing so now entirely because of her. They had agreed that he "was to handle entirely the matter of the anti-aircraft shell." He did handle it as well as he knew how, he wrote. "It has not been my fault that (a) it has not developed as I hoped, and (b) that they in Washington have not sent you personal notice of it." But "both you and Louis have made me feel, time and time again, as if it were somehow my fault that both (a) and (b) above did not materialize."

Upset by this distrust, Antheil continued, "I found it necessary for my peace of mind to come to explain to you and Louis that it was not possible to secure an invention's patent on these items, and to explain and justify my every step to date." In the beginning, he added, it had not been necessary to justify his actions. "You trusted me in the beginning," he told Hedy. "After awhile, and for some reason I shall not care to guess here, you do not trust me."

The previous evening, 9 January, he had gone to Hedy's house "just for amusement's sake" to "show you both how unjust you have been with me." What he did to show them is unrecorded, but whatever it was, Hedy responded badly. "I am terribly sorry," he wrote, "that you have taken it this way because, as you know fully well, I am terribly fond of you, and if things had only remained as they were in the beginning, I would have gotten much further along in all this business, long ago, probably." Which would at least seem to confirm that George and Hedy did not have an affair. Given George's history, Hedy may even have introduced Lou Eshman as a chaperone.

Antheil would inform Bullitt later that year that Hedy "is a queer girl [who] believes that spies and saboteurs are on every hand, and cannot understand why President Roosevelt does not immediately put them all under arrest. 'That is what we'd do in Europe' she insists, excitedly. I then have to patiently tell her that this is America, glorious Democracy, the ways of which are not always clear to the apprehensive European mind."

In the midst of their contretemps, on 23 December 1940, George and Hedy offered up their most important invention, which they identified at this early stage as "Idea for a Radio-Controlled Torpedo." The two "made blueprints, directions, explanations," Antheil wrote to Bullitt, "and sent them off to the National Inventors Council. They immediately showed interest in the project and asked for further explanation, which was duly sent."

The idea Hedy and George offered in this first iteration was not yet the Secret Communication System of their later patent, but the fundamental conception was in place. A ship would launch a torpedo, a plane would observe its trajectory; at regular intervals the plane would signal torpedo course corrections to the ship, and the ship would flash them to the torpedo. Between these isolated, brief signals, each sent on a different frequency, there would be radio silence among the three components of the system. So frequency hopping was included, but the hops were produced manually at intervals not of fractions of a second but of a minute or more. Not yet in place was the semiautomatic system using a modified player-piano roll that Antheil would contribute in the months ahead. But the two inventors' submission offered a beginning, and the first hint of what was to come. It was enough, evidently, to claim the interest of the council leaders.

Like Hedy and George's effort to invent a superior torpedo, the National Inventors Council had its beginnings in the torpedoing of a crowded passenger ship without warning by a German submarine. In the case of the National Inventors Council the ship was the Cunard liner *Lusitania*, torpedoed on 7 May 1915 as it was crossing from New York to Liverpool, with a loss of 1,134 lives, including more than 100 Americans. President Woodrow Wilson protested the sinking to the German Empire in the strongest terms; newspapers filled with stories of America's lack of preparation for a war made brutal by dark new inventions.

Early in July 1915, Thomas Edison expressed his opinion in a *New York Times* interview of what the government should do to foster invention in anticipation of joining the war. The secretary of the Navy, Josephus Daniels, a North Carolina lawyer and newspaper editor whose father had been a shipbuilder, read the interview and decided to enlist Edison's help in meeting the challenge. On 7 July he wrote the famous inventor a letter. After a long paragraph of flattery, it got to the point:

> One of the imperative needs of the Navy, in my judgment, is machinery and facilities for utilizing the natural inventive genius of Americans to meet the new conditions of warfare as shown abroad, and it is my intention, if a practical way can be worked out, as I think it can be, to establish, at the earliest moment, a department of invention and development, to which all ideas and suggestions, either from the service or from civilian inventors, can be referred for determination as to whether they contain practical suggestions for us to take up and perfect. . . .
>
> There is no particular place, or particular body of

men, relieved of all other work, charged solely with the duty of either devising new things themselves or perfecting crude ideas that are submitted to the department by our naturally inventive people.

The result of Daniels's effort was the Naval Consulting Board, organized in October 1915 with a large representation of inventors, engineers, and industrialists, a few mathematicians, and no scientists, a profession the self-educated Edison resented and preferred to avoid. After ragging the Navy about its "mentally inbred" officers, the Wizard of Menlo Park agreed to become the board's president. By the end of the war the board had reviewed more than 110,000 ideas and inventions, most of them submitted by ordinary Americans. Only about 110 passed the first two levels of preliminary examiners to be submitted to technical committees, and of those only one actually went into production, an instrument for testing pilots for airsickness. "Several others were developed," the board's historian writes defensively, "and might have later been used."

Despite this dismal performance by "our naturally inventive people," the Naval Consulting Board served as a model for the National Inventors Council that was organized by Secretary of Commerce Harry Hopkins, Franklin Roosevelt's close adviser, in the summer of 1940. Hopkins had been prodded to do so by a remarkable patent agent and theatrical producer named Lawrence Langner. Born in Wales in

1890, Langner trained as an engineer before becoming a patent agent for a London firm in New York in 1910. He left the firm in 1912 to represent the inventor and electrical engineer Charles F. Kettering. Kettering had just patented the first electric starter system for Cadillac; Langner represented him in securing patent protection in Europe. Success with that opportunity led Langner to set up in business in New York as a patent and trademark agent specializing in securing foreign protection for American clients.

The Welsh engineer was also interested in theater. He was one of the founders of the Washington Square Players, an ambitious amateur group that opened its doors in 1915; in 1919, as an outgrowth of the Players, he co-founded the Theatre Guild. Later in life, besides producing plays and musicals, Langner would co-found the American Shakespeare Festival Theatre and the Westport Country Playhouse, all while continuing work as a successful patent and trademark agent.

In the summer of 1940, Langner had discussed the problem inventors faced in dealing with the U.S. government with an engineering colleague, Thomas Midgley, the co-inventor with Kettering of leaded gasoline. (As a high-school baseball player in Ohio, Midgley had identified the diluted sap of the slippery elm as the best substance for pitching fast-curving spitballs; many professional pitchers took it up. Besides leaded gasoline he was the inventor of Freon, the refrigerant that contributed greatly to the creation of the ozone hole. An environmental historian would describe Midgley as having "had more impact on the atmosphere than any other single organism in Earth's history.") "Inventors often lost a great deal of time in trying to interest the Government in their ideas and inventions," a science journal summarizes Langner and Midgley's discussion, "because they did not know which agency would make use of them, and as a result often sent them to the wrong place. Of all the places chosen by inventors to send their brain-children the one most often selected was the office of the President of the United States, where there is no agency for dealing with them."

Kettering, like Edison before him a prolific inventor, agreed to chair the board of the new organization that Harry Hopkins assembled; Langner became board secretary, Midgley a board member. Thus positioned to respond to George and Hedy's invention were three men ideally prepared to see its virtues. Like Hedy, Langner was experienced with theater and an inventor himself as well as a patent agent. Midgley and Kettering, working with Elmer Sperry and a group of other engineers, had developed a remote-controlled, gyroscopically stabilized "flying bomb" during World War I that had reached the stage of field trials when the armistice ended the war in November 1918.

By mid-May 1941, Antheil could report to Bullitt, with some skepticism, the first indications of interest at the National Inventors Council in his and Hedy's torpedo:

And now we've received word from Mr. Langner, who is head [sic] of the council, and is in town, that he'd like very much to discuss the invention with us! Hedy and

I are very excited, and we're going to see him tomorrow morning at eleven. (Down in my shoes, however, I've an idea that perhaps Mr. Langner might only be interested in seeing how the beauteous Hedy appears in full life?)

Antheil was still smarting from his dispute with Hedy the previous winter; in his letter to Bullitt he made it ad hominem:

Hedy is incredibly childish about some things: for instance, she never learned how to write, either in German or English, although she speaks German, French, and English almost flawlessly. When she does write (I've caught her taking notes at our conversations) she writes phonetically—in all languages. She is an incredible combination of childish ignorance and stupidity— and definite flashes of genius.

Since Hedy dropped out of school at sixteen, it may be that she never learned to spell words by language. More probably, faced with writing in three or four different languages, she had applied her gift for invention and decided it would be faster and more efficient to write them all phonetically in the notes she made for her personal use. Certainly she wrote and spelled competently in public documents. George Antheil disliked being questioned, as Hedy and Lou

Eshman had questioned him, especially since he considered their suspicions unjustified. It also must have been difficult for him, despite his outward bonhomie, to spend time with a twenty-six-year-old woman who was living a life of wealth and fame while he scraped a living doing Hollywood hackwork in a community mostly unaware of his enlarging body of serious compositions—and while his beloved brother lay broken and dead beneath the North Sea, one of the first American casualties of what was still a European war.

Consistent with this analysis, Antheil invested at least as much time during the period when he and Hedy were working on their magnetic proximity shell and radio-controlled torpedo in promoting his theory of glandular criminality as a method potentially useful for analyzing the Axis leadership from afar. He pressed Bullitt for contacts, visited Washington for ten days at his own expense, and met with the FBI director, J. Edgar Hoover, members of Hoover's staff, and FBI technical experts. Hoover assured him he was "deeply interested," Antheil said, but nothing came of it. "I am very unhappy since my brother's death," Antheil appealed to Bullitt. "I feel that it is futile to attempt to do anything but help National Defense, nowadays. My mind is busy in a thousand directions; I have boundless energy, nowadays." He had cured himself of his "Parisian asthma," he believed, "through adrenal cortex [extract] and did not have a single cold all this winter and I WISH I could do something."

While Antheil was besieging Washington with glandular criminology between sessions at the drafting board with Hedy Lamarr, Hedy was filming *Ziegfeld Girl*, choreographed by Busby Berkeley, co-starring Judy Garland, Lana Turner, James Stewart, and Tony Martin. Shooting began in September 1940 and lasted until January 1941, coterminous with the conception of frequency hopping. The jeweled peacock-feather headdress Hedy wore in the film, one of her biographers writes, "became her trademark." It was an Adrian concoction, high camp, and one of his last; he left MGM in September 1941 to start his own business. Hedy, after filming *Ziegfeld Girl* by day and inventing by night, flew off to the Riviera early in the new year for a midwinter vacation. The British foreign secretary, Anthony Eden, was there; at his request, she briefed him on the state of European public opinion.

Hedy legally changed her name that winter, from Hedwig Kiesler to Hedy Lamarr. Her mother was now living with friends in London, and Hedy continued to pursue arranging her immigration. She also hired the Los Angeles legal firm of Lyon & Lyon to develop the Lamarr-Antheil patent application, which involved searching the records for possible prior knowledge and helping craft the most encompassing possible language.

Between 23 December 1940, when the two inventors submitted their first rough ideas to the National Inventors Council, and 10 June 1941, when they filed their patent application not merely for a radio-controlled torpedo but for a much broader, pioneering, and fundamental "Secret Communication System," Hedy and George constructively reduced their invention to practice. Doing so was necessary to win a patent, because a patent requires that novel ideas be embodied in a mechanism that works. But again crucially: the particular mechanism described in the patent application need be only illustrative, one of a number of possible embodiments. Hedy and George chose to embody their idea in a player-piano-like mechanism because they knew how to design such a mechanism, not because it was the only possible system that their idea would support.

"Langner seems to be deeply interested," Antheil wrote to Bullitt late in this second phase of invention development. "He promises to promote the matter with all possible vigor; he believes that it will work." Langner had arranged the connection with Samuel Stuart Mackeown, professor of electrical engineering at Caltech in Pasadena. "He requested Mackeown to get in touch with me and work out some additional details," Antheil wrote. "This was done, and Dr. Mackeown is now as enthusiastic about the torpedo anti-jam device as is anyone. He states positively that it will work."

NINE

Red-Hot Apparatus

In the proposal that Hedy Lamarr and George Antheil sent to the National Inventors Council in December 1940, there is an important final paragraph that hints at the next stage of development of the ideas they described:

> We are, at present, working upon a method of sending the radio signal from the sender-ship to torpedo which will incline to make it even more silent and undetectable than now, due to the actual sender-apparatus itself.

Around this time, Antheil carefully sketched and noted their "method" on two sides of an ordinary No. 10 office envelope. Their invention, he wrote, now consisted of "two sister system[s]," which he lists as "(1) Synchronized alternating radio wavelength devices for both sending ship and receiving torpedo" and "(2) Minimum broadcast time length device to double ensure torpedo against jamming." Number 2 was the system Hedy and George had presented to the National Inventors Council on 23 December that depended on limiting the transmissions to brief bursts between stretches of radio silence to limit enemy jamming. Number 1 was the new system they were working on in the winter and spring of 1941, which Antheil listed as "synchronized alternating"—that is, the transmitter and the receiver frequency-hopped together in synchrony.

Now, however, in his literally back-of-the-envelope diagram, Antheil added a crucial new concept: "ribbons" perforated with instructions to the torpedo about both the minimum-time sequence and the frequency-hopping sequence:

(a) The ribbon wavelength synchronizer runs its perforations continuously, allowing sender to broadcast at any time deemed necessary—and as often.

(b) The ribbon wavelength *alternator* synchronizer has a predetermined pattern—impossible to guess at by the enemy—since it insures a two-way lock against such possible jamming.

So the signal that passed between the ship and its torpedo would now not only be extremely brief but also hop from frequency to frequency. And the hopping would be not manually controlled but controlled by "ribbons," the general term Hedy and George were using here for a control device such as a player piano's scrolling roll of paper. Once again, their notations make it clear that they were thinking beyond the specific mechanism of the player piano to a more universal concept of analog control programmed with punched tape.

Antheil had faced a similar control problem when he attempted to synchronize player pianos, and the mechanism he now proposed for his and Hedy's invention was similar: using matching player-piano-like rolls of paper in transmitter and receiver with slots cut into the paper to encode the changes in frequency. As the slots rolled over a control head, they would actuate a vacuum mechanism similar to the mechanism in a player piano, except that instead of the operation culminating in a pushrod moving the piano action, it would culminate in pushrods closing a series of switches. The switches would be arrayed below the pushrods. Closing a specific switch would connect one of several differently tuned condensers—devices that store electric charge—to an oscillator. An oscillator is an electronic circuit that generates a regularly changing radio signal, called a carrier wave:

Each different condenser would impose a different frequency on the carrier wave—more cycles per second or fewer:

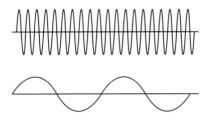

Antheil waggishly affirmed a range of up to eighty-eight frequency hops for the system, the number of keys on a piano—a musician's sly autograph.

With a signal hopping all over the radio spectrum, and doing so not regularly but arbitrarily, more or less at random, the transmission would be impossible to jam because an enemy would be unable to follow it. He might accidentally jam one frequency if the signal happened to hop there, but with a potential for hundreds of hops per minute, the transmission would lose very little information from such minor interference. Anyone listening on a single frequency would not even realize a signal was being transmitted, since he would hear, at most, only an occasional brief blip.

To make jamming even more difficult, George and Hedy

proposed using seven tuning condensers on the transmitter but only four on the receiver. Three of the transmitter channels would thus send a false signal, one with no operating function, further complicating any effort to determine which transmissions to jam. Antheil's hobby of inventing and breaking codes, which he had shared with his deceased brother, Henry, found application in this feature.

How much of the electronics of their invention Hedy and George designed themselves isn't clear from the available record. Obviously, the player-piano-like system was George's contribution. He also knew more than a little about radio electronics from his Hollywood experience recording his music for reproduction on sound film. "It's my daily work," he reminded Bill Bullitt once, "here in the studios, to know *everything* about microphones and sound-recording." Hedy's knowledge would have been whatever she had picked up during her years at the Mandl dinner table; as Antheil wrote to Bullitt, "Hedy was once married to a big Austrian munitions manufacturer and knows her munitions upside down." (In the same letter Antheil noted of their torpedo that it "can be guided over twenty miles by radio," which may have overestimated a torpedo's fuel capacity.)

An important additional component, not original, was a "novel torpedo steering device—infinitely more accurate—and based upon [the] Philco Remote Control principle." This electronic component would process the signals the torpedo received and convert them into instructions (in the form of electrical signals) to move the torpedo's rudder to port or starboard to steer the weapon toward its target.

Here, then, was the invention in its semi-final form. What remained in the spring of 1941 was conferring with Mackeown at Caltech about the electronics of the system and working with Lyon & Lyon, their patent lawyers, to prepare as broad a patent application as possible.

One problem that emerged to be solved was how to start both "ribbons"—the one in the transmitter and the matching one in the receiver—at the same time so that the information coded on the two ribbons would be synchronized. If the ribbons were not in sync, the receiver would be tuned to the wrong frequencies when the signals arrived and would fail to pick them up, so the requirement was crucial. Hedy and George's patent application explains the system they devised:

> It is of course necessary that the record strips . . . at
> the transmitting and receiving stations, respectively,
> be started at the same time and in proper phase relation
> with each other, so that corresponding perforations in
> the two record strips will move over their associated
> control heads at the same time. We therefore provide
> an apparatus for holding both record strips in a starting
> position until the torpedo is fired, and for then simulta-
> neously releasing both strips so that they can be moved
> at the same speed by their associated motors.

The holding apparatus in both transmitter and receiver used a pin that would engage a special starting hole in the record strip to begin moving the strip forward. A compression spring normally held the pin away from the starting hole. Below the pin was a solenoid—a wire-wrapped iron rod that was held away from the pin magnetically when the wire was electrified. The solenoids on both the transmitter and the receiver were connected by wire to a battery, and the current from the battery kept each solenoid energized. The battery circuit also connected to the transmitter in the ship and the receiver in the torpedo. When the torpedo was launched, it broke the connecting wire, which interrupted the electricity flowing to the solenoids, which ceased to be magnetized, which released the solenoid rods, which pushed up the pins that engaged the starting holes, which allowed the clock motors in both the ship and the torpedo to begin simultaneously moving the record strips.

A second problem Hedy and George had to solve followed from their decision to include seven transmitting channels in the transmitter but only four receiving channels in the receiver, thus allowing false signals to be sent on three channels to complicate and confuse an enemy's jamming efforts. Resolving this problem was simpler: they provided for an indicator light at the transmitting station that would flash whenever the units were in transition between frequencies but would stay lit when the three false channels were engaged.

With these problems solved and the Secret Communication System fully laid out in their patent application, Hedy and George filed with the U.S. Patent Office for patent recognition on 10 June 1941. Receiving a patent would be an achievement different, of course, from a decision by the U.S. War Department to take up their system and develop it for military use. Their patent effort worked through the Patent Office; their War Department effort worked through the National Inventors Council. The council's response continued to be positive, Antheil wrote to Bullitt on 30 June:

> Recent communications from the office of Lawrence Langner, who is chief of the National Inventors Council, indicate that they and the War Department are deeply interested in Hedy Lamarr's and my new radio-controlled torpedo; Langner indicates that the torpedo may be constructed and experimented with in Detroit. . . .
>
> In the meantime Hedy wants to come with me to Washington but I am discouraging this idea. We wouldn't come unless the War Department really wants our torpedo, which torpedo is (incidentally) unique in that it is "jam-proof."

Hedy was restless in part because she'd been laid off between pictures at MGM. She was ill in February and had lost weight; her illness ran into the layoff when she rejected the scripts she was offered. She was also in the process of negotiating a salary increase. "Hedy was here Sunday," Antheil wrote to Bullitt on 19 July, "and as you can imagine is very keen about the whole project, and she keeps calling me almost every day to see how it has progressed. . . . It so happens that you are, apparently, Hedy's dream prince. Some years ago she's [sic] apparently seen a picture of you somewhere or another and decided that you are 'it.' You'd better watch out for her if she ever comes down to Washington without us. She's rather inclined to, incidentally, as she is still on probation with M.G.M. and hasn't anything to do just now." An asterisk after "inclined to" led to a handwritten footnote: "Only concerning the invention, of course."

Early in the new year, Boski Antheil had confronted her husband over his continuing effort to make a killing writing motion-picture scores. She explained the background to the confrontation in her unpublished memoir:

> At that time George's music was not much played; we lived in Hollywood, and although George was working as much as ever on his symphonic music, as far as New York was concerned, he was corrupted because he did a few picture scores to make a living, he was tainted, and not only tainted but probably living in the lap of luxury, sold himself down the river, probably had a golden bathtub, swimming pool and surrounded by gin and chorus girls. If they only knew! How we had to struggle to make ends meet, juggling bills and

sometimes bill collectors, bringing up our son Peter, never really knowing where the next check was coming from. Mainly because George did not wish to become a movie composer, but reserved most of his time for his own music, and one picture a year or even two certainly does not keep the wolf away from the door.

"Hollywood is a funny place," Boski added. "If you don't play the game whole-heartedly and really live the Hollywood game, your price per picture is not very great." She confronted her husband, hoping to convince him that he should give up his schemes for making a killing so that he could return to serious composing, and she trumped her argument by pointing out that at that time, in early 1941, they had exactly $36 in the bank.

Antheil saw the point. "O.K.," he said. "Let's move away. I'm in a rut."

"We moved to a tiny little house on the beach," Boski remembered, "where we spent two very productive years, the sea and the air clean and windswept. Peter walking around barefooted winter and summer, me cooking big pots of soup, and many friends coming out there to visit us." The cottage was in Manhattan Beach, a few miles down the coast from what is now Los Angeles International Airport.

Antheil echoes his wife. "We got the smallest house . . . into which three humans can crowd. And all of a sudden, we were all very happy. We didn't have five dollars to buy groceries with, but we were happy." It was there that Hedy visited them, in an elegant white silk pantsuit, her rich, dark hair stirred by the breeze off the ocean, happy to spend time at the beach with normal people.

One day that summer Antheil walked to the Manhattan Beach post office, two miles away, and found a single letter in his box. "It was from my dead brother Henry's estate and contained a check for $450 [$7,000 today]. 'O.K., Henry,' I said into the air, 'I'm not so dumb but that I can't get this. You want me to go on with my work, and I'm going on.'" Boski's response to the gift was Hungarian. "His arm out of the grave!" she exulted.

Henry's gift added to the Antheils' reserve from a film George had worked on that spring, he told Bullitt in late July: "I have just finished a very large motion picture score for which I have made the producers pay three times what it was worth; consequently I am able this summer and early autumn to do nothing but my own work, and am turning back again to musical composition. I am just finishing my fourth string quartet."

Hedy was finally busy again at the beginning of August, playing the female lead opposite Robert Young in the film version of John P. Marquand's best-selling novel *H. M. Pulham, Esq.* For once she was cast not as a remote beauty but as a complex, vital woman, a New York advertising executive in love with a Back Bay Bostonian too proper to give up his settled marriage for love; later she would call it her favorite role.

By now she had made seven major American films and was a certified Hollywood star—a superstar, we would say today.

At the end of September, for reasons of its own, the National Inventors Council leaked the story of Hedy's inventive gifts, omitting Antheil entirely:

HEDY LAMARR INVENTOR

*Actress Devises "Red-Hot" Apparatus for
Use in Defense*

Special to the New York Times

HOLLYWOOD, Calif., Sept. 30—Hedy Lamarr, screen actress, was revealed today in a new role, that of an inventor. So vital is her discovery to national defense that government officials will not allow publication of its details.

Colonel L. B. Lent, chief engineer of the National Inventors Council, classed Miss Lamarr's invention as in the "red hot" category. The only inkling of what it might be was the announcement that it was related to remote control of apparatus employed in warfare.

By then Hedy and George's Secret Communication System had passed to the Navy for evaluation, which means it had cleared two layers of council examiners. Antheil told Bullitt that it "actually reached [Charles F.] Kettering, who was very enthusiastic about it and recommended it to the Navy." Kettering's enthusiasm may have prompted the announcement that the *New York Times* picked up.

The invention reached the Navy at a bad time. War with Japan was in the air in the autumn and early winter of 1941. On 3 November, the same day the United States began evacuating military and civilian dependents from the islands of Guam, Midway, and Wake, the U.S. ambassador to Japan, Joseph Grew, cabled Secretary of State Cordell Hull warning of the possibility of war:

> [In State Department paraphrase:] The Ambassador said it was his purpose to insure against the United States becoming involved in war with Japan through any misconception of Japanese capacity to plunge into a "suicidal struggle" with us. . . . It would be short-sighted to underestimate the obvious preparations of Japan; it would be short-sighted also if our policy were based on a belief that these preparations amounted merely to saber rattling. Finally, he warned of the possibility of Japan's adopting measures with dramatic and dangerous suddenness which might make inevitable a war with the United States.

Japan did adopt those "measures"; at 8:00 a.m. on Sunday, 7 December 1941, a flight of 353 Japanese carrier-based light bombers and other aircraft attacked the U.S. naval base at Pearl Harbor, Oahu, Hawaii, where a large part of the U.S. Pacific Fleet was anchored. Japanese bombs and aerial torpedoes sank or destroyed four American battleships; four others were hit and damaged. Three cruisers were also hit and damaged and three destroyers. The battleship *Arizona* was devastated by an eight-hundred-kilogram armor-piercing bomb; the bomb started an oil fire forward that initiated a chain of explosions culminating in the explosion of the ship's main magazine. Everyone belowdecks died: 1,177 men, the largest death toll on a Navy ship in U.S. history.

A seaman on the battleship *California*, Eddie Jones, described the devastation on the Pacific Fleet's flagship:

> When that big bomb blew up and they put the fire out,
> I looked down in that big hole that went down three or
> four decks. I saw men all blown up, men with no legs
> on, men burned to death, men drowned in oil, with
> oil coming out of their eyes and their mouth and their
> ears. You couldn't believe it was happening. You could
> see it in front of your eyes, but you couldn't believe
> it. Here it was, a beautiful day—a beautiful Sunday
> morning—and you see everything blowing up and
> ships sinking and men in the water. And you think,
> we're at peace with the world. This can't be happening.

The next day, 8 December, President Franklin Roosevelt spoke to a grim assembly of both houses of Congress. "Yesterday," he began, "December Seventh, Nineteen Forty-One, a date which will live in infamy, the United States of America was suddenly and deliberately attacked by naval and air forces of the Empire of Japan." He called for a declaration of war, which Congress immediately voted and he signed the same day.

Two days later, on 10 December, the Japanese invaded the Philippines. The United States had few ships in the area other than submarines and torpedo boats; these were deployed to patrol the region and attack Japanese shipping. "In the weeks and months that followed," write two American naval historians, "U.S. submariners began to realize that there was something wrong with their torpedoes. More often than not success against Japanese ships was denied by torpedoes that ran too deep, exploded too soon, did not explode at all, or did not have enough explosive power to sink a ship when they did engage and detonate." In 1942, 60 percent of U.S. torpedoes were duds. Japanese ships steamed into port with unexploded torpedoes stuck in their hulls like arrows.

It took the submarine service eighteen months to push past Navy bureaucracy, skepticism, and hostility to determine what was wrong with its torpedoes. The answer was, almost everything. In the years between the world wars, torpedo research and development at the Naval Torpedo Station in Newport, Rhode Island, had withered on an annual budget of only $90,000. Because Newport saved money by testing its torpedoes' depth meters with lighter practice torpedoes in still water, the weapons ran too deep, missing their targets entirely. Newport's secret magnetic exploder, which was supposed to serve as a proximity fuse, failed to detect an enemy ship more often than it succeeded, and frequently triggered an explosion soon after the torpedo had left its submarine. These and other problems, including the torpedo station's bitter and prolonged labor troubles, gave way only slowly to the determined assault of frustrated submarine commanders in the field.

Under the circumstances, the Navy had no interest whatsoever in developing a new torpedo with a complicated guidance mechanism; it would be happy simply to see its old-fashioned unguided torpedoes occasionally both hit their marks and explode.

Hedy and George heard of the decision months before their patent was allowed—in late January or early February 1942. "After considering our torpedo for a long while," Antheil wrote to Bullitt on 5 February, "(during which period it seems that it was almost accepted) the government declined our torpedo, saying that it was excellently worked out, but still somewhat too heavy. Miss Lamarr now insists that we get to work and lighten it."

Whether they did or not, the record doesn't reveal. By summer, Antheil was prepared to explain to Bullitt what he believed had gone wrong, an explanation worth quoting at length:

Hedy and I spent a lot of time—and money—design-
ing and perfecting [our torpedo]. It was then sent
in—and it actually reached Kettering, who was very
enthusiastic about it and recommended it to the
Navy.

But it was turned down at the Navy.

Now, Bill, I don't carp at that; God is my witness that if our Navy has something better than the
Antheil-Lamarr radio torpedo no one would be happier
than I. Honestly.

But it's the way they turned it down.

They said that the mechanism we proposed was "too
bulky to be incorporated in the average torpedo."

Now, if there's one single criticism they could not,
nor should not have made, it was THAT one.

Our fundamental two mechanisms—both being
completely, or semi-electrical—can be made so small
THAT THEY CAN BE FITTED INSIDE OF DOLLAR
WATCHES!

I know (or I think I know) why they said that. In
our patent, Hedy and I attempted to better elucidate
our mechanism by explaining that a certain part of it
worked not unlike the fundamental mechanism of a
player piano. Here, undoubtedly, we made our mistake.
The reverend and brass-hatted gentlemen in Washington who examined our invention read no further than
the words "player piano."

"My God!" I can see [them] saying. "We can't put a player piano into a torpedo!"

Or so it would appear. Remember that Kettering — who is quite a genius along the line of torpedoes —recommended it.

Our invention—had it been accepted—would enable a plane far above to steer a torpedo or A WHOLE FLEET OF TORPEDOES—against an enemy squadron, correcting and re-correcting their rudders from a single steering wheel in the plane—AND the enemy fleet could not POSSIBLY "jam" or "smear" this control. (This latter feature is our main contribution to already known and tested elements of the so-far useless radio controlled torpedo.)

The U.S. Patent Office had a better opinion of Hedy and George's invention than did the U.S. Navy. On 11 August 1942, it issued the two inventors U.S. Patent No. 2,292,387 for their Secret Communication System. Curiously, Hedy had filed not under her current legal name of Lamarr but disguised, as it were, as Hedy Kiesler Markey, as if she were determined not to allow her celebrity to influence the judgment of the patent examiners either way.

When the Navy acquired the patent to a technology it had formally rejected is a question that can't be answered until the National Inventors Council records are opened; they have remained off-limits now for decades on the grounds that they contain proprietary information. The Navy as well kept the technology secret for the next forty years, one reason Hedy and George's contribution long went uncelebrated.

After the patent was awarded, Antheil wrote to Bullitt again, complaining about the Navy's rejection of his and Hedy's inventions. Bullitt's influence had declined sharply in Washington, however. He had dreamed of becoming secretary of state. Antheil had even encouraged him to think of running for president as Roosevelt's successor. But Bullitt had destroyed his relationship with Franklin Roosevelt the previous year by pressing Roosevelt to dismiss Bullitt's archrival Sumner Welles, whom the Secret Service had reported drunkenly propositioning a series of annoyed African-American Pullman porters on a late-night train trip from Huntsville, Alabama, to Washington. Bullitt, writes George Kennan, "unquestionably dealt to his relationship with FDR a blow from which it was never fully to recover. Welles was a close personal friend of the Roosevelt family. The President never fully forgave Bullitt for what he regarded as an uncharitable personal vendetta—a vendetta pursued not just in this one highly unpleasant interview in the White House but in statements to other people which were not long in reaching the Presidential ears."

Beset with troubles, Bullitt had no influence to spare for George Antheil. "I am sorry you feel so frustrated about your torpedo idea," he responded on 25 August, "and wish I could do something to help you. I have, however, referred your idea to the proper people here and will take it up again. I am still learning the Navy from the ground up and, at the moment, can do nothing more."

By then, both Hedy and George had given up trying to change the Navy's mind. They had both moved on. Antheil settled in at Manhattan Beach to write symphonies; he composed his Third Symphony, he told Bullitt, "during the anxious days of midsummer 1942"—anxious because the Germans and the Japanese were on the advance and the Allies on the defensive in those early months of American engagement in the war—and began his Fourth Symphony that year as well. Boski said later that the new work had been her husband's creative "rebirth." His *Tragic* Symphony followed, as well as less ambitious compositions. Between 1940 and 1946, Antheil wrote no movie music at all, supporting his family by working behind the scenes as a news analyst for the journalists Manchester Boddy and John Nesbitt, employment which had followed from his book and articles predicting with remarkable accuracy the course of the war.

Hedy's war work took a more public direction, appropriately for a celebrity. Antheil had advised her at the outset of their partnership that she would serve the nation better selling war bonds than inventing. So had the Navy when it rejected the Secret Communication System. Evidently, Hedy decided to prove just how successful a salesperson she could be. While effectively out on strike from MGM in a salary dispute, she campaigned nationally with other movie stars to sell war bonds to raise money for the war. War bonds allowed ordinary citizens to feel they were helping with the fight while controlling inflation by removing money from circulation. They were sold in denominations from $18.95 ($260 today) up to $1,000 ($14,000 today), with ten-cent-savings-stamp books available to those who couldn't afford to buy an entire bond at once.

At the beginning of September 1942, at a luncheon in Philadelphia with a $5,000-war-bond minimum, Hedy told the group of businessmen and labor and social leaders to "chip in and help Uncle Sam win this war," adding, "I am just a plain gold-digger for Uncle Sam. I'm here to help win the war. I think you're here to see what that Lamarr dame looks like." Then, in what the *New York Times* reporter on the scene called "a serious tone," she went on:

> We should be here for the same purpose. What you think Hedy Lamarr looks like doesn't worry me as much as what Hirohito and Hitler are doing. Every time you dig in your pocketbooks you tell those two rotten men the Yanks are coming. Let's make the end of the war come soon. Don't think about what the other fellow is doing. You buy bonds!

And they did, $4,547,350 worth ($62,344,000 today) among them, with another $2,250,000 ($30,847,000) pledged at a "victory show" Hedy headlined at Philadelphia's Academy of Music that evening. Two days later, the *Times* reported, she knocked them dead in Newark:

> NEWARK, N.J., Sept. 4—Hedy Lamarr, motion-picture star, took Newark by storm when she arrived here today to urge the purchase of war bonds. More than 7,000 persons blocked her path when she emerged from the Robert Treat Hotel and, later, in Military Park, it took more than a score of policemen to control a crowd estimated to be between 15,000 and 20,000.
>
> Several women fainted. Hundreds of camera fans took pictures of the Hollywood celebrity.
>
> When Miss Lamarr rode along Broad Street in a jeep, bus passengers stood up to wave, motorists honked their horns and many youths attempted to reach her conveyance on bicycles. The crowds were too large to permit many direct sales of bonds, but a score of women volunteers experienced no trouble in obtaining signed pledges.

A young Walter Cronkite introduced her at a rally that evening in Trenton.

A week later, back in New York, Hedy stood with Mayor Fiorello La Guardia as he announced Carole Lombard Memorial Week. (The thirty-three-year-old actress, the wife of Clark Gable, had been killed in a plane crash the previous January on her way home from an Indiana war-bond rally.) By 14 September, when Hedy arrived back in Los Angeles, she had sold almost $25 million ($343 million) in bonds.

She found a more intimate opportunity to serve her adopted country in October when the newly organized Hollywood Canteen opened its doors. Bette Davis and John Garfield had organized the club with support from the Music Corporation of America. The Hollywood Canteen served military men and women in uniform—their admission ticket—most of whom were awaiting shipment overseas. Hedy worked there faithfully twice a week, typically wearing a dirndl skirt and blouse, dancing with the servicemen and washing dishes.

That year Bette Davis introduced her to the actor John Loder, another tall, handsome older man. Loder was English, Eton educated, the son of a British general, and a veteran of the bloody campaign at Gallipoli during World War I. They married in May 1943, when Loder was forty-five and Hedy was twenty-seven. The day before their wedding, Hedy presented her betrothed with a bill for $350 ($4,800 today), half the cost of his dinners at her house the previous month, including half the cook's salary. He was disconcerted at this sign that she meant to be financially independent but paid up.

It was a good marriage for a time, longer than most of Hedy's marriages, his second and her third. With her dispute resolved with MGM she was working again more than full-time; her films from the war years include *White Cargo* with

Walter Pidgeon, *The Heavenly Body* with William Powell, *The Conspirators* with Paul Henreid, and *Experiment Perilous* with George Brent and Paul Lukas. In 1945, the year her daughter, Denise, was born, Hedy made *Her Highness and the Bellboy* with Robert Walker and June Allyson.

And all the while her Secret Communication System patent gathered dust somewhere in a Navy Department file cabinet, itself a secret, due to expire seventeen years out, in 1959, seemingly of no use to anyone.

O *Pioneers!*

A broad and fundamental patent now existed for a frequency-hopping radio system. It had been constructively reduced to practice. It belonged to the U.S. government. The U.S. Navy, which found no immediate use for it, had filed it away. Since it was classified secret, the government denied its identifying information to those who had no need to know, including the names of the two unlikely patentees, Hedy Kiesler Markey and George Antheil.

A consulting engineer at Hoffman Laboratories in Los Angeles remembered encountering this Secret Communication System patent in the mid-1950s, when it was passed to him as the basis for a U.S. Navy contract project. The consulting engineer was a Michigan-born descendant of Polish nobility named Romuald Ireneus Ścibor-Marchocki, educated at Wayne State University and Caltech and twenty-eight years old in 1954. "When we received the contract to develop the

Sonobuoy," Ścibor-Marchocki recalled in an online tribute, "we were provided with a copy of the H. Kiesler-Markey [*sic*] patent. Since it was dated a decade previously, we assumed that it was an existing secret technology, devised by some clever electrical engineer, working under a Navy contract and thus obligated to assign the patent to the Navy."

Hoffman Laboratories manufactured military communication systems as well as consumer electronics. Ścibor-Marchocki was handed the Secret Communication System patent because the Navy had contracted with Hoffman to build a jam-proof sonobuoy based on the technology, and Hoffman assigned him to design it. "Sonobuoy" is a portmanteau of the words "sonar" (*so*und *na*vigation *a*nd *r*anging) and "buoy"; the device was to consist of a miniature sonar system built into a parachute-deployable buoy, intended to detect and locate an enemy submarine with sound waves and transmit the coordinates to a sub-chaser aircraft overhead.

In his tribute, Ścibor-Marchocki reconstructs his work on the Hoffman sonobuoy:

> As requested, we designed the radio communications following the concept of the [Markey-Antheil] patent. . . . To perform the frequency-hopping, we would have employed a cylinder (spool) with protrusions. Each frequency would have been assigned an individual follower [contact] riding in a row parallel to the axis of the cylinder. There would have been perhaps a dozen frequencies. How fast would the cylinder

rotate? . . . 90 rpm sounds about reasonable. Anything slower would compromise security. The Sonobuoy and the listening aircraft would employ the same [type of] spool. When the aircraft wanted to listen to a different Sonobuoy, it would have to change spools.

"In retrospect," Ścibor-Marchocki adds, "I realize that the Navy asked us at Hoffman (and me in particular) to design a frequency-hopping radio system; because they considered that if anybody could, we would. Thus, rather than existing technology, this was intended to investigate a new (but neglected) concept."

The sonobuoy that Ścibor-Marchocki designed was a narrow cylinder like a length of pipe about two feet long that floated perpendicular to the water surface with a hydrophone suspended below it on a cable. It was meant to be dropped in multiples of at least three in a pattern that would allow the sub-chasing aircraft to triangulate the submarine's location. It "worked very well as a listening device," Ścibor-Marchocki writes, "and for either active or passive ranging of submarines, but it was not practical as a system." It was impractical, among other reasons, because it drifted from its assigned position and was difficult to locate precisely in those days before GPS; its hydrophone was jostled excessively in rough seas; and the spinning frequency hopper aboard the sub-chaser plane required constant adjustment to stay in sync with the one in the sonobuoy. The system could have been improved, but the Navy came up with a system better suited to its purposes of permanently anchored hydrophones connected to a shore station by cable.

That system, Ścibor-Marchocki notes, "solves each of the foregoing [sonobuoy] problems. Regrettably, without the necessity of radio communication, there was no more spread-spectrum involved. To this day, the Navy has hydrophones deployed along the whole coast of the USA." (The broader and more general term "spread spectrum" began to be substituted for "frequency hopping" in the early 1950s. Frequency hopping is a specific kind of spread spectrum; another kind, "direct sequence," involves electronically or digitally spreading the signal across a wide bandwidth, making it largely indistinguishable from noise.)

Ścibor-Marchocki's testimony directly links the Markey-Antheil patent to a specific postwar technology, but a number of other developments in frequency-hopping military communications preceded Hoffman's sonobuoy work. The high-level classification imposed on such work makes it impossible to determine if the engineers involved benefited directly from knowledge of Hedy's idea of frequency hopping. What at least is clear is that none of that work preceded Hedy and George's invention.

The University of Southern California electrical engineering professor Robert A. Scholtz examined the origins of spread-spectrum communications at length in a paper published in 1982, just as the technology was becoming available for civilian development. He told me he was aware of the Markey-Antheil patent, and a colleague, Robert Price, interviewed Hedy for a follow-up paper published in 1983. ("Lamarr and Antheil," Price writes, "seem . . . to have been more than a score of years ahead of their time, considering that [frequency hopping] evidently was not used operationally against intentional jamming until [1963].") Scholtz devotes several pages to a discussion of what he calls the "prehistory of SS communications," most of which concerns the development of radar. None of these earlier developments constitute a complete frequency-hopping system such as Hedy and George's.

Curiously, the most direct predecessor that Scholtz identifies to later spread-spectrum developments was a radio control system for a glide bomb developed during World War II not by Germany but by the U.S. Navy with support from the National Bureau of Standards. The parallel between German and U.S. glide-bomb work raises the interesting question of whether the Navy had learned of German glide-bomb development from the Oslo Report or some other espionage source. If so, it has never acknowledged a connection. "One of several secure radio guidance efforts," Scholtz writes of the U.S. program, "took place at Colonial Radio, predecessor of the Sylvania division at Buffalo, NY. This project was under the direction of [the engineer] Madison Nicholson."

Nicholson's team had developed a limited two-hop frequency-hopping system, code-named Janus, to help foil possible jamming of the glide-bomb radio link. "Although the radio link was designed to be covert," Scholtz notes, "the system could withstand jamming in one of its two frequency bands of operation and still maintain command control." The Navy glide bomb that eventually emerged, code-named Bat, saw limited use in the Pacific theater late in the war, sinking several Japanese ships and destroying bridges and other targets in Burma.

An important postwar influence on spread-spectrum development was a seminal paper by the mathematician and electrical engineer Claude Shannon, "A Mathematical Theory of Communication," published in the *Bell System Technical Journal* in 1948. In his paper, which has been called the founding document of information theory, Shannon showed that a wider spectrum—a wider channel—can carry a given quantity of information more reliably than a narrower channel. An English expert puts it another way. "Shannon's formula," he writes, "indicates that a wide-band signal is more robust [than a narrow-band signal] when the channel is noisy and, of course, jamming is just another source of noise." Another advantage of wider bandwidth compared with narrower, Shannon showed, is that the same volume of data can be sent with a less powerful transmitter. (Shannon coined the term "bit" in his 1948 paper as well.)

In 1955, contemporary with Ścibor-Marchocki's sonobuoy work at Hoffman Laboratories, Madison Nicholson at Sylvania Buffalo initiated work on a radio communications system that Sylvania hoped would be selected for the new nuclear submarines the Navy was developing. Known by the acronym BLADES, the system used frequency-hopping spread spectrum (FH-SS) to overcome the problem of multipath distortion in long-range communications—that is, distortion caused by a signal bouncing off mountains and other radio-reflective surfaces and arriving at a receiver along several different paths at once.

After several years of testing and improvement, a prototype BLADES was delivered to the Navy in 1962. The prototype was installed on the *Mount McKinley*, the flagship of the Navy's amphibious forces during the Cuban missile crisis that October. Scholtz writes that the radio system was "evidently carried into the blockade associated with the Cuban Missile Crisis but was not tested there due to a radio silence order." The *Mount McKinley* sailed from the Caribbean to the Mediterranean early in 1963. There, says Scholtz, "intentional jamming was encountered, and BLADES provided the only useful communication link for the *McKinley*. Thus, BLADES was quite likely the earliest FH-SS communication system to reach an operational state."

Between 1945 and 1978, the U.S. military and national security agencies developed a number of different secret communication systems based on various forms of spread spectrum. Among these were a secure radioteletype system for the U.S. Army; a remote-control system for the Corporal rocket; radio guidance systems for the Sergeant and Jupiter missiles, abandoned when inertial guidance was chosen instead but transferred over to the U.S. Air Force's Deep Space Program for telemetry, command, tracking, and ranging; the Phantom radio system developed by General Electric for the Air Force; the Martin Company's RACEP system that provided secure mobile voice communications for up to seven hundred users; a similar system from Martin called Cherokee; Motorola's MUTNS tactical navigation system; ITT's SECRAL missile guidance system; and a half dozen others. In 1978, Scholtz notes, the U.S. National Security Agency declassified and allowed to proceed through the patenting process "scores of patents including at least a dozen on SS techniques."

Romuald Ścibor-Marchocki, having moved to Aerojet-General in the early 1960s, also made further use of spread-spectrum technology as system manager for a surveillance drone. The drone, he writes, "eventually flew over Vietnam." He personally designed the two-way radio system for the drone, which was implemented digitally rather than in analog form, as previous incarnations of frequency hopping had been. "For the first time, we had the ability to switch frequencies rapidly; thus, we called it 'spread-spectrum.' It is the same concept as 'frequency-hopping,' only performed much faster. . . . The radio signal required very little transmitter power and was immune to noise and interference from other drones, which would employ the exact same carrier frequency." In Ścibor-Marchocki's drone radio design is thus the basis for a solution to a problem that would reemerge with the advent of the cellular phone: allowing many different phones to talk at once by arranging for them to hop in many different sequences, thus staying out of each other's way.

———

Since all these developments were secret, Hedy and George remained unaware of them. Their patent expired seventeen years out from its awarding, in 1959. George Antheil, the bad boy of music, expired with his patent that year of a heart attack on 12 February at the age of fifty-eight. His 1945 autobiography, *Bad Boy of Music*, had been a best seller, and then he had seen his music finally succeed in the years after the war; in 1947 he was counted among the top four most performed American composers, in company with Samuel Barber, Aaron Copland, and George Gershwin.

Antheil had returned to musical drama in the last decade of his life: an opera, *Volpone*, based on the Ben Jonson play; one-act operas, *The Brothers*, *Venus in Africa*, and *The Wish*; a ballet based on Ernest Hemingway's short story "The Capital of the World"; a cantata, *Cabeza de Vaca*; songs, sonatas, and film, television, and radio scores. "It is a wonderful feeling," he wrote to his fellow composer Kurt Weill, "to once more, in my imagination at least, be living back in the theater. It is 'home.'" George and Boski had remained together and close in their intimate, complicated marriage; when George died, in New York City, he left behind not only Boski and Peter but also an illegitimate six-month-old son.

Virgil Thomson's review of Antheil's Fourth Symphony,
first performed in 1944, catches something of Antheil's brash
character as well as the spirit of his music:

> There is everything in it—military band music,
> waltzes, sentimental ditties, a Red Army song, a fugue,
> eccentric dancing—every kind of joke, acrobatic
> turn, patriotic reference and glamorous monstros-
> ity. It is bright, hard, noisy, busy, bumptious, efficient
> and incredibly real. It is "Columbia, the Gem of the
> Ocean" orchestrated in red, white, and blue, with three
> cheers for the same every five minutes and plenty of
> pink lemonade. By moments it is thin of texture, but
> at its best and busiest it makes a hubbub like a live
> crowd and five military bands. And its tunes can all be
> remembered.

George Antheil had traveled far from his early cacopho-
nous avant-garde work. He might well have said of his life, as
of his music, that he had come home.

———

The birth of her daughter, Denise, in 1945 had left Hedy with
psychosomatic pain, for which she began seeing a Boston psychoanalyst. Flying from Hollywood to Boston for treatment
"became a shuttle trip," she remembered. Traumas emerged
from earlier in her life: a schoolgirl encounter with a flasher;

a workman's sexual assault when Hedy was fourteen that she had kept secret from her parents out of shame; exposure to a frightening scar, from his rib cage to his hip, that Anthony Eden had revealed when he came aboard in swim trunks to swim with Hedy in the south of France. Two years later, "time and analysis" had helped her. "I found out who I am," she said. Part of her problem had been the uncertainty and defensiveness she had felt in "the crisp, competitive world of Hollywood." Even so, she was one of the few European artists who had successfully transitioned from her native culture and language to America. By 1947 she was ready to remake her life.

Believing that she could find better scripts if she had a wider range of choices, she negotiated past Louis B. Mayer's angry possessiveness to extricate herself from MGM. Analysis had changed her, and her marriage to John Loder now felt lonely. "It was the case again," she recalled, "where the unknown had much more allure for me than what I had now. I wanted a divorce, feeling there were other more exciting, more interesting experiences waiting for me." First, however, she wanted another child, because she remembered the loneliness of her own childhood and hoped to spare Denise similar isolation. (She had essentially disowned James, her adopted son.) Anthony John Loder, Denise's younger brother, was born in March 1947. Three months later Hedy divorced her third husband.

She was less successful making films on her own. "My

judgment on scripts was faulty," she concluded. "I was embarrassed . . . and worried." Out of that limbo, in 1949, Cecile B. DeMille chose her to play Delilah in his costume blockbuster *Samson and Delilah* opposite Victor Mature. The picture premiered in New York on 21 December and broke all box-office records. Afterward, having fought with DeMille on the set about costume and character, Hedy was delighted with the seasoned director's assessment of her. "We argued quite a bit," he told a radio interviewer, "but I respected Hedy. She loves picture-making, it shines out of her. I had no idea Hedy was as good an actress as she turned out to be. She was fiery, yet did everything expected of her. When I was blowing up, Hedy remained calm. She had great self-confidence and self-respect. Considering her reputation and beauty, she is a most unaffected person."

As her film roles declined in the 1950s, Hedy began working in the new medium of television, although more frequently as a celebrity guest than as an actor. By about 1970 she had given up that work as well. The careers of Hollywood stars, especially women, can be as short as the careers of professional athletes. Hedy's career in film and television spanned more than thirty years. She estimated she had earned $30 million or more from acting—$372 million today. Financing films and submitting to voracious California community property laws across six divorces consumed most of it; she lived far more modestly in the later decades of her life than she had in her years of Hollywood stardom.

Spread-spectrum technologies emerged from government secrecy in 1976 with the publication of the electrical engineer Robert C. Dixon's textbook *Spread Spectrum Systems*, which a Dixon colleague called the "first comprehensive, unclassified review of the technology" that "set the stage for increasing research into commercial applications."

Commercialization was further encouraged by President Jimmy Carter's inflation czar, Alfred E. Kahn, a Cornell economist best known for deregulating the U.S. airline industry while chairman of the Civil Aeronautics Board in 1978. Kahn, a liberal Democrat, promoted government deregulation for economic reasons, believing that it spurred economic development—a cause later taken up with conservative ideological fervor by President Ronald Reagan. At the Federal Communications Commission between 1977 and 1981, chairman Charles D. Ferris, a Boston-born physicist and attorney, abandoned the usual FCC practice of finding a consensus with the electronics industry before changing or adding to FCC rules. Instead, in line with Carter and Kahn's emphasis on deregulation for economic growth, Ferris looked for innovative technologies hampered by what his assistant Michael J. Marcus calls "anachronistic technical regulations." There was a reason for the regulations, Marcus explains:

In the 1970s the spectrum technology area was highly concentrated, with only a few major manufacturers:

Western Electric was the near-exclusive supplier of the local and long distance telecommunications industry, cellular was in its experimental stage, and the regulatory status quo was rather acceptable to the small "club" of major manufacturers serving the US market, all of whom were domestic companies. While regulations prevented rapid innovation, it [*sic*] also generally prevented both new entrants and technological surprise from the few competitors. Products could be planned and introduced with assurances that the R&D costs could be amortized over a long sales period. It was a cozy oligarchy for the major manufacturers, but it denied the public the benefits of rapid introduction of new technologies and services just as in the parallel Bell System telecommunications monopoly.

Ferris set out to change the situation, beginning with a study the FCC commissioned, delivered in December 1980, titled *Potential Use of Spread Spectrum Techniques in Non-government Applications*. Its key finding: "Spread spectrum techniques offer a unique method of sharing a common band between multiple users without requiring the users to coordinate their transmissions in any way." For technical as well as political reasons, the report raised the possibility of using what are called the ISM bands—the radio frequencies allocated to industrial, scientific, and medical uses other than communication (such as microwave ovens and equipment for medical diathermy and industrial heating)—for spread-spectrum radio. Such equipment generated radio noise that interfered with narrow-band radio transmissions, which was why it had been allocated frequency bands of its own. (They were also called the garbage bands.) Spread spectrum, however, was resistant to such interference just as it was resistant to jamming. And since radio spectrum is limited, any new technology that could be overlaid onto spectrum already assigned to other transmissions without interfering with those transmissions was of obvious benefit. Or so Ferris and Marcus hoped.

The benefits were less obvious to competing interests within both government and industry. Marcus felt as if he were advancing into a lion's den in 1983 when he went to the National Security Agency to make his case. "It became clear," he writes, "that some individuals at NSA hoped to keep spread spectrum off the commercial market for fear that foreign military use of the technology would complicate NSA's signal intelligence responsibility." Fortunately for him, the wife of the "very senior NSA official" who introduced him had just bought a new car with a scanning AM/FM radio, a technology similar to spread spectrum, which meant, he told the assembled, that "the spread spectrum Pandora's box may already have been opened and that shutting it was probably futile." After that fortuitous rescue, Marcus writes, opposition to civil spread spectrum within the U.S. military and intelligence communities began to fade.

The communications industry was not so easily persuaded. Television networks and manufacturers such as RCA and General Electric feared that spread spectrum would interfere with television signals. Manufacturers of cordless phones, which today use spread spectrum almost exclusively, suspected a plot by the FCC to deny them the narrow channels they preferred by dumping spread spectrum onto them.

Once the FCC understood the industry complaints, it forged an acceptable solution by authorizing spread spectrum in the ISM garbage bands, and then at low (but adequate) wattage. At the same time, and crucially, the commission allowed spread-spectrum communications in those bands to operate *without an FCC license*, unregulated. That meant that inventors, entrepreneurs, and manufacturers could proceed from conception to market without having to slog through the long, legally complicated, and therefore expensive process of seeking FCC approval. ("Legend has it," Marcus notes, "that the original unlicensed device was a 'couch potato'—like remote control for radio receivers." So the 1939 Philco Mystery Control once again revealed its originality.)

If all this bureaucratic infighting seems obscure, what followed from it is happily familiar. "The rules adopted," Marcus writes, "had a much greater impact than any of [their] advocates could ever have imagined at the time. They enabled the development of Wi-Fi, Bluetooth, the majority of cordless phones now sold in the US, and myriad other lesser-known niche products." The Global Positioning System (GPS) uses spread spectrum. So does the U.S. military's

$41 billion MILSATCOM satellite communications network. Wireless local area networks (wLANs) use spread spectrum, as do wireless cash registers, bar-code readers, restaurant menu pads, and home control systems. So does Qualcomm's Omni-TRACS mobile information system for commercial trucking fleets. So do unmanned aerial vehicles (UAVs), electronic automotive subsystems, aerial and maritime mobile broadband, wireless access points, digital watermarking, and much more.

A study done for Microsoft in 2009 estimated the minimum economic value of spread-spectrum Wi-Fi in homes and hospitals and RFID tags in clothing retail outlets in the U.S. as $16–$37 billion per year. These uses, the study notes, "only account for 15% of the total projected market for unlicensed [spectrum] chipsets in 2014, and therefore significantly underestimates the total value being generated in unlicensed usage over this time period." A market of which 15 percent is $25 billion would be a $166 billion market.

Hedy followed these developments. Sometimes she felt bitter about her lack of recognition as an electronic pioneer. In 1990, when she was seventy-five, she told a reporter for *Forbes* magazine how she felt. "I can't understand," she said, "why there's no acknowledgment when it's used all over the world." The reporter noted that she was "six times divorced and now living in Miami on a Screen Actors Guild pension" and couldn't help feeling she'd been wronged. "Never a letter," Hedy added, "never a thank you, never money. I don't know. I guess they just take and forget about a person."

Yet she didn't let her resentment consume her. Robert Osborne, the journalist and television host, recalled her enthusiasm for life in a late profile:

Few people were ever blessed with a merrier sense of humor, few sailed through the calamities of life with more of a blithe spirit, few apologized less frequently and seemed to be having more fun, even when the bloodhounds were snapping at her ankles. The Hedy I had known since 1963 was game for anything—a picnic, a charade party, a dress-up affair at [the restaurant] "21," a walk on the beach or a climb over a "No Admittance" barricade to get a look at something she was curious to investigate. Her energy, curiosity and generosity were enormous. . . . She was colorful without attempting to be and constantly unpredictable. . . . A sad figure? No way, and certainly not to the lady herself. She neither complained nor apologized. Hedy embraced that "Auntie Mame" philosophy that "life is a banquet." If there was any tinge of tragedy connected to Hedy Lamarr, it was the fact that she ever had to grow old. When a face had been as flawless and celebrated as hers, it's not easy greeting birthdays. . . . So Hedy retreated from the gazes of those who didn't look deeper. She avoided cameras, shut the doors, kept out of sight, filled her days with activities (and lawsuits) and, with the humor still intact, tolerated the rest of us.

One man who never forgot about Hedy was a retired U.S. Army colonel named Dave Hughes. Hughes, a highly decorated veteran of both the Korean and the Vietnam Wars who lives in Colorado Springs, had retired early from the Army to explore the developing world of wireless digital communications. Something of a maverick, the descendant of eleven generations of Welsh Calvinists, he got interested in setting up free digital wireless for rural schools that couldn't afford the high cost and charges of dedicated T1 lines strung out forty or a hundred miles across the Colorado prairie. "I wasn't worried about rural kids getting a computer," he told me. "They were falling in price and were going to be cheap. The problem was going to be the cost of communications and the evil empires called the phone companies."

Hughes determined to solve that problem, at least by demonstration. He set up the first computer bulletin board in Colorado Springs, "two-way with a Hayes modem." He helped Montana link up its 114 one-room schoolhouses with FidoNet, the noncommercial network of linked bulletin boards established by the San Francisco artist, pioneer hacker, and self-styled anarchist Tom Jennings in 1984. Then the National Science Foundation heard about Hughes's work and came calling. After the NSF investigated, it awarded Hughes a seven-year, $7 million grant to continue exploring digital wireless for rural education. And it was while Hughes was doing due diligence for his NSF grant work, investigating the prior art, that he came across the story of Hedy Lamarr and frequency hopping.

By then, Hughes was connected to the burgeoning digital community in the San Francisco Bay Area through the Well, Stewart Brand's pre-Web, dial-in version of a linked digital community, and he reported his discovery there. In 1993 he received a Pioneer Award from the Electronic Frontier Foundation, a San Francisco–based nonprofit that defends digital rights and celebrates electronic pioneering. In 1994, attending an IEEE award ceremony for Mike Marcus, the FCC's champion of spread spectrum, Hughes was irritated to hear Marcus say that Hedy's invention was never reduced to practice. "I told him I questioned that," Hughes says. "Because by this time, Ścibor-Marchocki had heard about my discovery and put two and two together. He'd contacted me and told me about his sonobuoy."

Hughes, a battle veteran with a Distinguished Service Cross who fell in love with Hedy Lamarr when he was thirteen, smelled sexism in the engineering community's casual dismissal of her contribution. He decided she deserved recognition for her pioneering invention of frequency-hopping spread spectrum. The award he settled on trying to win for her was the Pioneer Award from the Electronic Frontier Foundation, the same award he had received in 1993. (Other recipients: Doug Engelbart, Robert Kahn, Paul Baran, Vint Cerf, Linus Torvalds, pioneers all.) By then, it was 1996. He had become a familiar figure on the Well, and when he reported what he was doing, he says, and explained to the young people who Hedy Lamarr was, "there was a groundswell starting on the Well to endorse the nomination." He located Hedy's son Anthony in Los Angeles. The EFF voted the award, to honor George Antheil posthumously as well. Hedy herself was happy to hear of it—"it's about time," she told Anthony—but was unwilling to appear in public to receive it. The EFF agreed that Anthony, now fifty years old and a Los Angeles businessman, could do so on her behalf.

The ceremony was held on the evening of 12 March 1997 at an Electronic Frontier Foundation conference in Burlingame, outside San Francisco. Receiving the Sixth Annual Pioneer Award, Hedy spoke briefly through a recording her son had made. Dave Hughes, always resourceful, had also brought a recorder and caught the message on tape. When I visited him in Colorado Springs in 2010, he played the tape for me, and I heard Hedy's clear, Austrian-accented voice. "In acknowledgment of your honoring me," she said simply, "I hope you feel good as well as I feel good about it, and it was not done in vain. Thank you."

Eighty-two at the time of that long-delayed recognition, she sounded remarkably young.

[TOP] Hedy Kiesler (Lamarr), shown here at six, was born to wealth and privilege in Vienna in 1914.

[LEFT] Hedy's father, Emil, a banker, encouraged her interest in how things worked.

[ABOVE] The Kieslers entertained Vienna's cultural elite in their spacious apartments.

[LEFT] At sixteen, Hedy skipped school and talked her way into work at Vienna's largest film studio. Bit parts followed.

[BELOW] A first starring role in the 1933 Hungarian art film *Ecstasy* gave Hedy a controversial breakthrough.

[BOTTOM] Arms merchant Fritz Mandl, the third-richest man in Austria, married Hedy in 1933. The marriage soon soured.

[TOP] When arson destroyed his family's factories, Mandl rebuilt and sold munitions to Italy and Nazi Germany.

[LEFT] Mandl's power intrigued Hedy, but his possessiveness made her feel locked in a golden prison.

[BOTTOM] While hosting German experts at this Mandl hunting lodge, Hedy heard talk of torpedo technology—and remembered it.

[TOP LEFT] Young American composer George Antheil scandalized 1920s Paris with his radical music.

[MIDDLE LEFT] Igor Stravinsky, pictured here with premier danseur Vaslav Nijinsky, encouraged Antheil's work.

[BOTTOM LEFT] Antheil scored his notorious *Ballet mécanique* for bells, sirens, an airplane propeller, and synchronized Pianolas.

[BELOW] Antheil's complex, percussive scores required multiple player pianos.

Wireless Box Runs Radio by Remote Control

A radio receiver in the living room may be operated from the kitchen, a bedroom or any other part of the home with the aid of a small remote-control cabinet which has no wires leading to the receiver or any other physical connection with it. Since it is unnecessary to "plug in" the portable control unit or to attach it to the receiver, it is as easy to play the radio while sitting on the front porch as when in the living room beside it. With the aid of the wireless box, a Philco receiver designed for this form of remote control can be operated from a distance or tuned with controls built in the cabinet, whichever is handier. With the remote-control unit, any one of several stations can be selected, a change can be made from one station to another, volume can be adjusted or the set can be turned off, simply by operating a dial in the top of the wireless box. The makers claim each unit will operate only the set for which it is designed. While this is the first time wireless remote control has been applied to a commercial radio receiver, a tractor was operated by radio at Chicago's Century of Progress and wireless units have also been employed to control model boats, automobiles and airplanes. In the latter cases, the remote-control units usually consist of battery-

The radio receiver, above, can be operated from any room in the home with the aid of the remote-control box which is not connected by wires or in any other physical way with the receiver

operated radio oscillators transmitting high-frequency impulses. These controlling impulses actuate relays which operate the mechanism in the various devices.

Soilless Farm Yields Vegetables for Wake Island Colony

Passengers and crew of the trans-Pacific "Clipper" planes and the maintenance force on Wake Island dine there on fresh vegetables produced on the island's soilless farm. In ten days recently the shallow, water-filled trays yielded thirty-three pounds of tomatoes, twenty pounds of lettuce, twenty pounds of string beans, fifteen pounds of squash and forty-four pounds of corn. Lacking soil but favored by tropical weather, Wake Island was found to be an ideal place for hydroponic farming, in which essential minerals in water take the place of soil.

[TOP] German submarine wolf packs decimated British shipping in the early years of World War II.

[ABOVE RIGHT] Now in Hollywood and horrified by German sinking of transports carrying British children, Hedy determined to invent a counter-weapon: a radio-controlled torpedo that would randomly switch frequencies to avoid jamming.

[ABOVE LEFT] The first commercial wireless remote control gave Hedy a model for her torpedo control system.

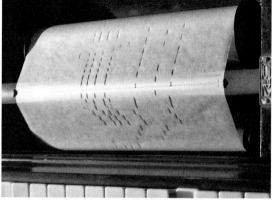

[TOP] George Antheil helped Hedy develop her frequency-hopping idea (left to right: unknown, Boski Antheil in striped dress, Hedy, George, unknown).

[ABOVE] From his player-piano experience, Antheil proposed using a punched "ribbon" to program frequency hopping.

[LEFT] U.S. torpedoes were plagued with accuracy problems until late in the war. In 1942, 60 percent were duds.

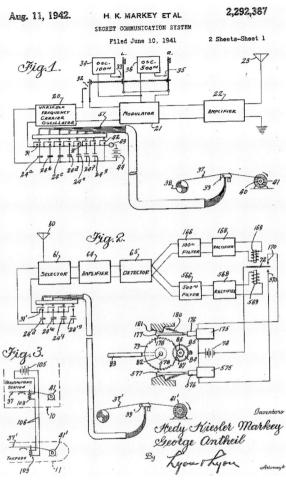

Fig. 1.

Fig. 2.

Fig. 3.

Inventors

Hedy Kiesler Markey
George Antheil

By *Lyon & Lyon*

Attorneys

[LEFT] Despite its torpedo problems, the U.S. Navy rejected Hedy and George's guidance system—too bulky, the navy brass said.

[BELOW] Hedy volunteered weekly at the Hollywood Canteen. In two weeks on tour in 1942 she sold $25 million in war bonds.

WESTERN EUROPE EDITION

THE STARS AND STRIPES

Unofficial Newspaper of U.S. Forces · In the European Theater

Vol. 2—No. 128   1 Fr.   Monday, Nov. 19, 1945

Hedy Adds New Twist to War

Actress Invents Control Device While Toying With Torpedo Idea, Has Patent to Prove It

Hedy Lamarr

HOLLYWOOD, Nov. 18 (AP).— It could not have been a press agent's stunt, because the timing was too perfect, but the report from London that film actress Hedy Lamarr had patented a radio steering device for torpedoes at least had a patent to back it up.

In an interview, Hedy modestly admitted she did only "creative work on the invention," while the composer and author, George Antheil, "did the really important chemical part."

Hedy was not too clear about how the device worked, but she remembered that she and Antheil sat down on her living room rug and were using a silver match box with the matches simulating the wiring of the invented "thing".

She said that at the start of the war "British fliers were over hostile territory as soon as they crossed the channel, but German aviators were over friendly territory most of the way to England.. I got the idea for my invention when I tried to think of some way to even the balance for the British. A radio controlled torpedo, I thought would do it."

Hedy asserted that the "control" device works on aerial as well as submarine torpedoes.

She said it works on anything and added that it was "lots of fun planning the invention and watching them pick, sort and put together all the little thingamabobs that went into the device." She said it was lots more fun being scientific than going to the movies.

She coyly dodged a query as to whether any company was interested in producing the device but did admit that as far as she knew nobody has ever used it yet for any practical purpose.

[TOP] *Stars and Stripes* made gentle fun of Hedy's invention, but within a decade it became basic military technology.

[ABOVE] Today Hedy's invention serves millions through GPS, Galileo, and GLONASS satellites, Bluetooth, cell-phone, and digital wireless systems.

[LEFT] Hedy (here at forty-six with her son and daughter, Anthony and Denise Loder) finally received recognition for her fundamental invention in 1997.

Afterword

Boski Antheil remained in Los Angeles after her husband's death, raising their son, Peter. Over the years she worked on writing a memoir of their life together, especially their Paris days. She wrote vivid scenes, some of which I've quoted in this book, but never connected them into a coherent narrative. Nor did she live long enough to enjoy the rediscovery of her husband's work, which began in the 1990s when *Ballet mécanique* was finally produced in something close to its original form with the aid of digital controls, some of them spread spectrum. Since then, George's mechanical ballet has been performed in many different venues, once using robot performers. When the American composer John Adams was writing the music for his 2005 opera, *Doctor Atomic*, and wanted to invoke the intersection of physics and war that resulted in the invention of the first atomic bombs, he intentionally scored the overture in the style of *Ballet mécanique*. Other Antheil works have become part of the modern classical canon.

The beginning of an essay Boski drafted in the late 1960s recalls her characteristic voice and connects her past and present:

Some time ago my son Peter, who is in his thirties, asked me when I first came to America. He is a great devotee of the Twenties and at that time he was particularly interested in vintage cars. When I told him that it was in 1927 (the occasion being the Carnegie Hall performance of George's *Ballet mécanique*), he exclaimed:

"It must have been wonderful to see all the old cars!"

I couldn't help laughing.

"But Peter, *then* they were *new* cars!"

And so it goes. Even though at times I feel like a vintage car myself, as most of my contemporaries are passing away, somehow the past seems as present to me as if it happened yesterday. It is hard for me to imagine that I am an ancient relic of the Twenties. I really don't feel that old, unless I suddenly realize that I am talking of a period about forty to forty-five years ago.

I get along with young people very well, in fact. Especially the kids in their early twenties, as they seem to be more related to the "20's," more in rapport with it. In a way they are trying to do pretty much what our generation was trying to do. The after-war generation wanted to deny the existing order, disillusioned and disgusted with the bourgeois generation responsible for the 1st world war and all its middle-class values. We really wanted to start the world from scratch . . . and believe me, when you are very young, this seems to be a very real possibility.

Boski Antheil died in 1978, Peter Antheil in 2010.

Fritz Mandl successfully escaped Austria after the *Anschluss* and immigrated to Argentina, where he became an Argentine citizen and manufactured munitions and light aircraft for the dictator Juan Perón. (He also invested in a minor Hollywood film company, Gloria Pictures, although he does not seem to have attempted to cast his former wife in a film.) During World War II the British Foreign Office, concerned that U.S. business interests might collude with Mandl to monopolize the postwar South American arms trade, set out to smear the Austrian parvenu as a Nazi sympathizer.

"To neutralize Mandl," writes a Canadian historian, "British diplomats adroitly manipulated the FBI and the anti-Mandl faction of the [U.S.] State Department; these Americans in turn manipulated public and official opinion in the United States. The campaign was successful: by mid-1945, Mandl had been swept from the board." After a 1955 treaty between the Western powers and the Soviet Union restored Austria to sovereignty, he returned to his native country and reclaimed his Hirtenberg empire, supplying the Austrian army and, later, such clients as Bolivia, Guatemala, Uruguay, and the United Arab Emirates. He died in 1977, roundly despised but seemingly possessed of a golden passport.

Hedy continued to receive honors after the Electronic Frontier Foundation's Pioneer Award. The Austrian Association of Patent Holders and Inventors awarded her its Viktor Kaplan Medal in 1998. An exhibition, *Hommage à Hedy Lamarr*, toured Austria in 1999.

"Hedy's fondness for invention remained with her until the end," writes her biographer Ruth Barton. "She had a proposal for a new kind of traffic stoplight and some modifications to the design of the Concorde [the Anglo-French supersonic passenger airliner that flew from 1976 to 2003]. There were plans for a device to aid movement-impaired people to get in and out of the bath, a fluorescent dog collar, and a skin-tautening technique based on the principle of the accordion. To the end of her days, she could perform devastatingly complex card tricks."

Her last residence was a three-bedroom house in Casselberry, Florida, north of Orlando. She moved there in October 1999. That same month, in *Vanity Fair*, she answered a "Proust questionnaire"—an old European parlor game that the magazine had revived. Her idea of perfect happiness, she answered, was "living a very private life," her real-life heroes Franklin Roosevelt and Winston Churchill. She was happiest "between marriages." Her favorite fictional hero was the scofflaw child Bart Simpson of the television cartoon series *The Simpsons*, and like Bart her motto was, "Do not take things too seriously."

Hedy's final goal in life was to live into the new millennium. As with movie stardom, wartime fund-raising, and pioneering invention, she persevered and achieved what she set out to do; she died alone at home in Florida, in her sleep, on the night of 19 January 2000. She was eighty-five years old. She left her children an estate valued at $3 million, most of it won in court settlements against corporations that tried to exploit her name and image and through shrewd stock investments. Her son and daughter, Anthony and Denise, carried her cremated remains back to Austria, as she had requested, and scattered them in the Vienna Woods on the slope of a hill overlooking her native city. There she rests today, high above the wide Danube valley where Marcus Aurelius wrote his *Meditations*, one with the trees and the grasses.

Acknowledgments

This book emerged from discussions at meetings of the Alfred P. Sloan Foundation book committee and with Sloan programs vice president Doron Weber. A grant from the foundation supported the work of research.

Hedy Lamarr's daughter, Denise Loder-DeLuca, was generous with her time and enthusiasm. Sheila Weller introduced us. Hedy's son, Anthony Loder, scanned vital documents for me and reviewed them with me at a time of grave illness. I value their confidence and hope that the result warrants it.

Nino Amarena, inventor, electrical engineer, and man for all seasons, tutored me in hydrogen peroxide technology, radio control, frequency hopping, the pleasures and frustrations of invention, and much more. His knowledge and guidance have been invaluable.

Dave Hughes gave me a day and evening to explore his nomination of Hedy for an Electronic Frontier Foundation award and his own electronic pioneering. Susi Maurer not only guided me around Vienna but also located and drove me to one of Fritz Mandl's hunting lodges, where we peered in windows and interviewed locals who remembered stories their parents told them of Hedy's isolation and loneliness there. Stanford University librarian Mike Keller and his staff at the university libraries were unfailingly helpful. Tara C. Craig of Columbia University's Rare Book & Manuscript Library located an important letter for me. My daughter, Katherine, drove me to Los Angeles to interview Anthony Loder.

At the Naval Undersea Museum in Keyport, Washington, curator Ron W. Roehmholdt briefed me and my grandson Isaac on torpedoes. Director Bill Galvani not only drove us to the ferry slip after our visit but also arranged to provide me with a copy of the Mark 14 torpedo manual. Meredith Peterson of the Congressional Research Service located a Washington-based researcher for me, Andrew Marchesseault, who skillfully assembled a large file of George and Boski Antheil writings and correspondence at the Library of Congress. John Adams was kind enough to answer several musical questions. Gerd Zillner at the Frederick and Lillian Kiesler Private Foundation in Vienna confirmed Frederick Kiesler's distant relationship to Hedy. Claudette Allison organized permissions with her usual skill.

Gerry Howard has been my supportive and collegial editor at Doubleday, his assistant, Hannah Wood, a patient, thorough hunter of photographs, rights, and permissions.

Ginger Rhodes read every word, more than once.

Notes

ONE: A CHARMING AUSTRIAN GIRL

7   spring of 1931: *The Weaker Sex* opened under Reinhardt's direction on 8 May 1931 at the Theater in der Josefstadt, Vienna.

7   "Are you here too" . . . "I took this as a mandate": Weller (1939), 69.

8   "Hedy had only the vaguest" . . . "Watch me look": Ibid.

8–9   "I had a little stage" . . . "from printing presses": Quoted in Shearer (2010), 12.

9   "She has always had": Quoted in ibid., 10.

9   "I underemphasized": Quoted in Barton (2010), 13.

9   son and daughter only learned: Anthony Loder and Denise Loder-Deluca, personal communications.

9   Freud's daughters: Barton (2010), 12.

10   twenty-one districts: As of 1910. The number today is twenty-three.

10   "a city of a thousand": Zweig (1943), 39.

10   "Precisely because the monarchy": Ibid., 21.

11   "The whole city": Ibid., 25.

11   "It was not the military": Ibid., 22–23.

12   "I acted all the time": Hall (1938), 24.

12   "in keeping with the Viennese" . . . "audience": Zweig (1943), 51.

12   "He made me" . . . "He had encouraged": Hall (1938), 21, 72.

13 "I knew that the studio": Ibid., 72.

13 *Geld auf der Strasse*: Lamarr misremembered which film in several later interviews, but *Geld* was released in November 1930 and is the only film that fits the chronology. I've corrected related facts such as her role and the director's name. For a complete filmography, see Shearer (2010), 360–90.

13 "Well, it was not too bad": Hall (1938), 72.

14 "were much more difficult": Lamarr (1966), 17.

14 "Reinhardt made me read": Ibid., 18.

14 "When you dance with her": Weller (1939), 69.

15 "It was at the rehearsal": Ibid.

15 "Almost before we knew it": Ibid., 70.

16 "who simply recoiled": Ibid.

16 "I've never been satisfied": Hall (1938), 72.

16 "decided for herself": Weller (1939), 70.

16 Alexis Granowsky: Barton (2010), 22.

16 "Excellent work": Quoted in Shearer (2010), 26.

17 "When I had this opportunity": Hall (1938), 73.

17 "I could not go": Ibid.

18 "I went to Prague": Quoted in Shearer (2010), 27.

20 "The world began": Zweig (1943), 152–53.

20 "This health and self-confidence": Ibid., 153.

21 "I don't want to become": Quoted in Horak (2001), 34. The source of this statement as Horak lists it is contemporary: the journal *Mein Film* 356 (1932), 10.

22 Vienna premiere: Barton (2010), 35.

22 "artistic" . . . "I wanted to run": Lamarr (1966), 30, 31.

22 "My mother and father suffered": Hall (1938), 73.

22 "the courtship of the young": "Sissy in Vienna," *Time*, 2 Jan. 1933.

23 "At first I felt": Hall (1938), 73.

23 "She looks wonderful": Quoted in Barton (2010), 46.

23 "From the first night": Hall (1938), 73.

24 ammunition factory in Hirtenberg: See Mötz (2010).

24 "he had negotiated": Newton (1986), 545.

24 "He introduced himself": Hall (1938), 73.

24 "a young viveur": "Latin America: Double Cross?" *Time*, 16 April 1945.

25   "He was so powerful": Hall (1938), 73–74.

25   "He asked me to go": Ibid., 74.

26   "I began to feel attracted": Ibid.

27   "small and quiet": Ibid.

27   "Almost at once": Ibid.

27   "Democracy is a luxury": "Latin America: Double Cross?"

28   "try to track down": Hall (1938), 74.

28   "nearly $300,000": "Cinema: The New Pictures," *Time*, 25 July 1938.

28   "it became one of the": Hall (1938), 74.

28   "I knew very soon": Ibid.

29   "prison of gold": Ibid.

TWO: BAD BOY OF MUSIC

30   to Europe in 1922: "In early 1922 I became a concert pianist, and traveled with my impresario, M. H. Hanson, to Europe where I was an immediate success." "Autobiographical Notes," box 14, folder 5, Antheil Collection, Library of Congress.

30   "a cello-sized man": "Music: Antheil's Fourth," *Time*, 28 Feb. 1944.

30   "He did nothing but write": Hecht (1964), 158.

30   "When I first went": Quoted in Antheil (1945), 2.

31   "Curiously enough": "The American Composer's Heritage," 1–2, box 14, folder 1, Antheil Collection.

31   "I myself was present": Ibid.

32   "When I was 17": "Why 'Bad Boy of Music'?" box 14, folder 7, Antheil Collection.

32   "I told him I was broke": Antheil (1945), 19.

32   "one of the richest": Quoted in Ford (1987), 8–9.

33   "on the basis": Bok to Antheil, 28 Sept. 1934, George Antheil Correspondence files, Library of Congress.

33   "In this way": Antheil (1945), 10.

33   "the exact duplicate": Antheil to Van H. Cartmell, 30 Sept. 1944, Correspondence files, Antheil Collection.

33   two tours: Ford (1987), 12.

34   "to either Italy": Antheil (1945), 9.

34   "the day she had disappeared": Ibid., 11.

34   "first, I wanted to learn": Untitled essay beginning "In 1922, as a young American composer," box 14, folder 14, Antheil Collection.

35   "the girls and wives": Antheil (1945), 26–27.

35   "There were just too many": Ibid., 27.

35   "George was a tremendously": Boski Antheil memoir, 10–11, box 17, folders 1–3, Antheil Collection.

36   "Thereafter, for two straight months": Antheil (1945), 33.

36   "about mechanistic": George Antheil, "MAMA!" datelined Paris, April 1, 1925, box 14, folder 8, Antheil Collection.

36   "You play my music": Antheil (1945), 40.

37   "an enormous fur coat": Ibid., 46.

37   "I happened to be born": Boski Antheil memoir, 9.

37   "dark, had high cheekbones": Antheil (1945), 49.

37   "related to various": Ibid., 50.

38   Jean Wiener: Stravinsky (1936), 110.

38   "She represented much": Antheil (1945), 86.

39   "everybody was terribly poor": Boski Antheil memoir, 10.

39   "When I later": Antheil (1945), 90.

40   "We arrived in Paris": Boski Antheil memoir, 8.

40–41   "which I gave up" . . . "none of which": Stravinsky (1936), 104–5.

41   "In contrast to her brother": Ibid., 102.

41   "Absolutely breathtaking": Boski Antheil memoir, 17.

41   "When I went to school": Ibid., 71.

41   "Paris was like a carnival": Ibid., 8, 17.

42   "I still don't remember": Ibid., 18.

43   "she was kind": Hemingway (1964), 35.

43   "threw up the job": Walsh (2010), 87.

43   "I tried my best": Ibid., 93.

43   "Sylvia and George immediately": Boski Antheil memoir, 18.

44   "was on the look-out": Imbs (1936), 23.

44   enclosed mezzanine: Ibid.

44   "consisted of one room" . . . "one went to the public": Boski Antheil memoir, 20, 40.

45   "I was very shy": Ibid., 20.

45   "the great piano warehouse": Antheil (1945), 104.

47   "In order to prevent": Stravinsky (1936), 101.

48   "the next day we went": Antheil (1945), 104.

48   "Months later": Ibid., 107.

48–49 "tremendously" . . . "for where": Ibid., 107–8.

49   "We are done": Antheil (1924).

49   "A dark, pretty": Antheil (1945), 121.

50   *Le coeur à barbe:* See Delson (2006), 47–49.

50   "All the celebrities": Quoted in ibid., 48.

51   "One day a tall": Quoted in ibid., 49.

52   "Even though the idea": Boski Antheil memoir, 6. Boski's recollection argues against Antheil's claim in *Bad Boy of Music* that he conceived his *Ballet mécanique* first and then "sought a motion-picture accompaniment to this piece" (134).

52   "George was writing": Boski Antheil memoir, 32(55).

53   "Georgette Leblanc": Monnier (1976), 247–48.

53   "the theater, the famous": Antheil (1945), 7.

53   "The uproar was such": Boski Antheil memoir, 28.

54   "I now plunged": Antheil (1945), 133.

55   "After the finish": Quoted in Whitesitt (1983), 19.

55   "Satie came out": "Why 'Bad Boy of Music'?", 1.

56   "where Antheil played": Copland and Perlis (1984), 75.

56   "My first big work": Quoted in Oja (2000), 80–81.

THREE: MECHANISMS

57   "Mr. George Antheil was engaged": Quoted in Donald (2009), 44.

57   "during the winter": Antheil (1945), 137.

58   "Kiesler liked it so well": Boski Antheil memoir, 61, box 17, folders 1–3, Antheil Collection, Library of Congress.

59   "One night we went": Ibid., 65.

59   "Bullitt is a striking man": Kennan (1985), 57.

59   "a hearty, charming": Imbs (1936), 103.

60   "And of course there was Bill": Boski Antheil memoir, 60–62.

61   "He was furious": Brownell and Billings (1987), 112.

62   "Bill and Louise": Boski Antheil memoir, 60–62.

62   "We had a lovely": Ibid., 44.

63   "One day in the future": "The Death of Cities," box 14, folder 3, Antheil Collection.

63   "We went to Vienna": Boski Antheil memoir, 66–67.

64   "Fritz was immersed": "Latin America: Double Cross?" *Time*, 16 April 1945.

64   "are unintelligible": Sedgwick (1939), 282.

65   "The only serious problem": Ford (1987), 42–43.

65   "This is the first edition": Quoted in Whitesitt (1983), 22.

66   "The idea of [sixteen] pianos": George Antheil, "My *Ballet méca-nique*," 10 June 1951, box 14, folder 8, Antheil Collection.

67   "There was a great deal": Imbs (1936), 100–2.

69   "We shall see": Quoted in Lehrman (1999). Translation corrected from the original German version in *De Stijl*, 8 June 1924, 101–2.

70   two thousand player pianos: Mick Hamer, "Don't Shoot the Pianola," *New Scientist*, no. 1435/1436, 20–27 Dec. 1984, 52.

70   "And what will the music": George Antheil, "An Introduction to the Actuality of My Present Music," Ezra Pound file, box 1, folder 88, Antheil Collection.

71   "When I first came": Boski Antheil memoir, 110.

72   "The eleven grand pianos": Friede (1948), 52.

72   "Everybody wanted to meet": Ibid., 55.

72   "The trouble was": Ibid., 56.

73   "When it reached": Ibid., 60–61.

74   "The unheard-of viciousness": Antheil to Bok, [April 1927], box 2, folder 1.17, Antheil Collection.

74   "This year I made": Ibid.

74   "heartsick and broke": Antheil (1945), 197.

75   "America has received": Antheil to Bok, [April 1927], box 2, folder 1.17, Antheil Collection.

76   "I changed my musical style": Antheil, "Autobiographical Notes," box 14, folder 5, Antheil Collection.

76   "The place was well calculated": Antheil (1945), 265.

FOUR: BETWEEN TIMES

79   armed with surplus weapons: Mötz (2010), 56.

79   "The *Heimwehr* and its principals": Newton (1986), 545.

79   "Austria may be assured": Quoted in Johnson (1934), 126.

80   "Mandl also sold arms": Newton (1986), 545.

80   armed both sides in the Spanish Civil War: Ibid.

80   "He would often ask" . . . "Sometimes he would get": Hall (1938), 75–76.

81   "Soon I knew" . . . "and in these blue violets": Ibid., 75.

81   "we entertained": Ibid.

82   "the Jew, Mandl": Joseph Goebbels, speech delivered at National Socialist Party Congress, Nuremberg, 1937.

82   "I did not do more": Hall (1938), 75.

82   "Any girl can be": Schickel (1962), 212.

82   "There were times": Hall (1938), 75.

83   "My husband would sit there": Ibid.

83   "but both times": Ibid., 76.

83   "But still he did not" . . . "I was out driving": Ibid.

85   "in his last agony": Ibid.

85   "I wore black": Ibid.

85   "From the moment": Ibid., 76–77.

85   It might even take blackmail: As Lamarr recounted in a conversation with the engineer and inventor Carmelo "Nino" Amarena in 1997. Nino Amarena interview with author, 5 Jan. 2011.

85   She would have to be a sponge: Nino Amarena: "Hedy told me: 'I was being a sponge because I had to find a way to escape Mandl—even blackmail if necessary. And all I had to do was pose and listen.' " Ibid.

86   "Things were pretty tough" . . . "We also had the roof": Boski Antheil memoir, 99, box 17, folders 1–3, Antheil Collection, Library of Congress.

87   "We are around": George Antheil, "My Father," June 1945, box 14, folder 8, Antheil Collection.

88   "Bill told me": Antheil (1945), 270.

88   "a whole coterie": Ibid. On the premiere of *Helen Retires*, see invitation in MS 112, box 3, folder 42, William C. Bullitt Papers, Yale University Library.

88   "Bewildered, I stopped composing": Autobiographical notes, box 14, folder 5, Antheil Collection.

89   "pure Paris" . . . "an American ballet": Antheil (1945), 276.

89   "I had to accept": Antheil to Bok, 22 Sept. 1934, George Antheil Correspondence with Mary Louise Curtis Bok, 1921–40, Library of Congress.

90   "MacArthur and I lured": Hecht (1962), 162–63.

90   "100% music": Antheil to Bok, 22 Sept. 1934.

90   "in a 'Russian' village": Antheil (1945), 272.

90   "With us were gypsy dancers": Hecht (1962), 163–64.

91   "This summer has been": Antheil to Bok, 22 Sept. 1934.

93   *My dear George*: Bok to Antheil, 28 Sept. 1934, Antheil Correspondence with Bok.

94   "wherein I *had* to represent": Antheil to Bok, [28] Sept. 1934, Antheil Correspondence with Bok.

95   "We had been discussing": Antheil (1945), 274.

95   "FOUR THOUSAND DOLLARS!": Ibid., 275.

FIVE: LEAVING FRITZ

98   "to drive a submarine": Walter (1954), 166.

99   hydrogen peroxide: See Walter (1947), Walter (1954), and Wernimont et al. (1999).

99   "only isolated suggestions": Walter (1947), 2.

100   "Years later": Walter biography, The Hellmuth Walter Web Site, www.walterwerke.co.uk/hw/wbiog.htm, accessed 22 March 2011.

100   Tests at the Chemical State Institute: Walter (1954), 166.

100   "After the encouraging": Ibid.

100   four-man mini-sub: Stokes (1998), 4. Another source, www.walterwerke.co.uk, mentions a three-man crew.

100   one thousand kilograms of thrust: Walter (1954), 166.

101   "The first flight": Ibid., 166–67.

102   Henschel Hs 293A: Bollinger (2010), 15; Piccirillo (1997), 9.

102   "could operate on any": Piccirillo (1997), 4.

103   "He was very interesting": The interviewer was Nino Amarena: Nino Amarena interview with author, 5 Jan. 2011.

105   "I felt more and more": Hall (1938), 77.

105   " 'Went walking' ": Tims (2003), 92.

107   "Hedi is expected": " 'Ecstasy' Star to Quit Rich Mate for Stage," *New York Sunday News*, 19 Sept. 1937, 3C.

108   "I cannot tell": Hall (1938), 77.

109   "At a small evening party": Ibid., 77–78.

110   "I saw *Ecstasy*": Lamarr (1966), 38–39.

110   "on board ship": Ibid., 41, 43.

111   "We all agreed": Hall (1938), 78.

III   "[Mayer] didn't like Kiesler": Walter Reisch in McGilligan (1991), 222.

SIX: CINEMOGLING

114   "She swam": "Cinema: The New Pictures," *Time*, 25 July 1938.
115   "The film and especially": Horak (2001), 34–35.
115   Man Ray recalled playing chess: Man Ray (1963), 296.
116   "My favorite thing": Hall (1938), 78.
116   "Howard Hughes once lent": Meeks (1990), 136.
116   tissue-box attachment: Denise Loder-DeLuca, personal communication, Nov. 2010.
116   "My life has been": "Backstage with Esquire," *Esquire*, Jan. 1939, 36.
117   "very very ill": Antheil to Bullitt, 18 June 1938, William C. Bullitt Papers, Yale University Library.
117   "almost died": Antheil to Bok [Month obscure, 1936; letter begins "Boski and I have at last reached California."], George Antheil Correspondence with Mary Louise Curtis Bok, 1921–40, Library of Congress.
118   "Ten years ago": Antheil (1935), 62.
118   "just enough of a taste": George Antheil radio interview, transcribed by Charles Amirkhanian, 28 Sept. 1980, box 14, folder 14, Antheil Collection, Library of Congress.
119   "I have been down": Antheil to Bok, [Oct. 1937], Antheil Correspondence with Bok.
119   three-score contract: Antheil to Bok, [Oct. 1937].
119   "liked the idea": Antheil (1945), 305.
119   "studied the writing field": Ibid.
120   "*but I no longer*": Ibid., 306.
120   *Every Man His Own Detective*: Antheil (1937a).
120   "a system" . . . "every last piece": Antheil to Bullitt, 18 June 1938.
120   Dutch challenger: Ibid.
121   "Our company": Antheil to Bullitt, 13 Aug. 1938, Bullitt Papers.
121    $49,000 . . . "little Peter": Antheil to Bok, 21 May 1938, Antheil Correspondence with Bok.
122   "The publishers of the world": Quoted in Bok to Antheil, 10 July 1938, Antheil Correspondence with Bok.

123 "We tried to keep up": Boski Antheil memoir, 96–99, box 17, folders 1–3, Antheil Collection.

124 "on the walls": Ibid., 99.

124 desperate financial crisis: Antheil to Bok, 18 Feb. 1939, 6 March 1939, 30 March 1939, 6 Feb. 1940, 28 March 1940, 16 March 1940. Antheil Correspondence with Bok.

124 "[We] put our meager": Boski Antheil memoir, 100–101.

125 "just making it on time": Ibid., 101.

126 "falsified assignment cables": Johnson and Hermann (2007), 50.

127 "mysteriously exploded": Quoted in ibid., 46.

127 "no hope is held": Hull to Antheil, telegram, 22 June 1940, box 18, folder 5, Other Correspondence, Antheil Collection.

128 "a brilliant raconteur": Quoted in Barton (2010), 90.

128 "We decided late Friday": Quoted in ibid., 81.

128 already bought a house: Ibid.

128 She told the court: Ibid., 90–91.

128 October 1939: Ibid., 83.

129 "I really wanted": Quoted in Baker (2009), 213.

130 "[German] Naval High Command": Dönitz (1959), 58–59.

131 "On her second day": Nagorski (2006), 20.

131 "Four days, 600 miles": U.K. Wartime Memories Project.

132 She began thinking: As she told Nino Amarena in 1997; Nino Amarena interview with author, 5 Jan. 2011.

SEVEN: FREQUENCY HOPPING

133 "We were good friends": Boski Antheil memoir, 94, box 17, folders 1–3, Antheil Collection, Library of Congress.

133 "a few homes": Powdermaker (1950), 21.

133 "to visit my heartbroken": Antheil to Bullitt, 18 Aug. 1940, William C. Bullitt Papers, Yale University Library.

134 the week when George and Hedy finally met: "Boski wasn't present, as she was visiting Mother and Dad in Trenton." Antheil (1945), 329.

134 "One day": Ibid., 327.

135 "eyeballs sizzled" . . . "The thing is": Ibid., 328–29.

136 "high up": Ibid., 329–30.

136 "We began talking": Ibid., 330.

136   "very, very bright": Ibid., 332.
136   "overheard him": Ibid., 330.
137   Hedy told an interviewer: The interviewer was Nino Amarena;
      Nino Amarena interview with author, 5 Jan. 2011.
138   "Here, then, and at long last": George Antheil draft text attached
      to Antheil to Lamarr, 10 Jan. 1941, 11, box 2, folder L, Antheil
      Collection, Columbia University Rare Book and Manuscript
      Library.
138   "Our pal, Ted Mills": Antheil to Boski, 12 Sept. 1940, box 18,
      folder 6, Antheil Collection.
139   "I have been up": Ibid.
139   "Boski was so indignant": Antheil (1945), 331.
140   "I have been a very": Antheil to Boski, 8 Sept. 1940, box 18, folder
      6, Antheil Collection.
140   "when Hedy moved down": Antheil (1945), 332.
141   "By the way": Antheil to Boski, 2 Feb. 1945, box 18, folder 6,
      Antheil Collection.
141   "I get around": Antheil to Bullitt, 30 Sept. 1940, Bullitt Papers.
142   "We talked like": Amarena interview with author, 5 Jan. 2011.
143   Philco console-model radio: Ramirez (2006).
145   generates high-frequency signals: See Miessner (1916), 137–44.
145   Formal German development: My source for this discussion is
      Bollinger (2010).
146   used a Walter hydrogen-peroxide rocket: Ibid., 15.
146   "More often than not": Amarena interview with author, 5 Jan.
      2011.
147   "hopping of frequencies": Ibid.
147   "Antheil and my mother": Meeks (1990), 137.
148   "I didn't know how": Amarena interview with author, 5 Jan.
      2011.
148   "doing me the honor": Antheil (1945), 291.
148   "that she and Antheil": "Hedy Adds New Twist to War," *Stars and
      Stripes*, 19 Nov. 1945, 1.
149   "In a radio communication": Markey and Antheil (1941), 21.
150   "An invention is the result": Quoted in Berle and De Camp (1937),
      4.
150   "An invention is not complete": Quoted in ibid.
151   "The invention is not the specimen": Ibid., 197.

153 "It seems that Hedy": George Antheil draft text, 11–12. Antheil
     Papers.

154 "We are, at this instant": Antheil to Bullitt, 16 Oct. 1940, MS
     112, box 3, folder 42, William C. Bullitt Papers, Yale University
     Library.
156 "split-second": "Idea for a Radio-Controlled Torpedo," 2, 23 Dec.
     1940, document in possession of Anthony Loder, Los Angeles.
157 "In the meantime": Antheil to Lamarr, 10 Jan. 1941, Antheil
     Papers.
158 Oslo Report: See Frithjof Sterrenburg, *The Oslo Report 1939—
     Nazi Secret Weapons Forfeited.*
159 "was to handle": Antheil to Lamarr, 10 Jan. 1941, box 2, folder
     7, George Antheil Papers, Columbia University Rare Book and
     Manuscript Library.
159 "I found it necessary": Ibid.
160 "is a queer girl": Antheil to Bullitt, 20 May 1941, MS 112, box 3,
     folder 42, Bullitt Papers.
160 "Idea for a Radio-Controlled Torpedo": Document dated 23 Dec.
     1940, in possession of Anthony Loder, Los Angeles.
161 "made blueprints": Antheil to Bullitt, 20 May 1941.
162 "One of the imperative": Scott (1920), 286–87.
163 October 1915: Ibid., 13.
163 "mentally inbred": Quoted in McBride (1992), 7.
163 more than 110,000 ideas and inventions: Ibid., 12.
163 only one actually went into production: Scott (1920), 125.
163 testing pilots for airsickness: National Inventors Council (1943),
     387.
163 "Several others": Scott (1920), 124.
164 "had more impact": Quoted in Michael Bess, review of *Some-
     thing New Under the Sun: An Environmental History of the
     Twentieth-Century World* by J. R. McNeill, *Journal of Political Ecol-
     ogy* 9 (2002).
165 "Inventors often lost": National Inventors Council (1943).
165 "And now we've received": Antheil to Bullitt, 20 May 1941.
166 "Hedy is incredibly": Ibid.

167   "deeply interested": Antheil to Bullitt, n.d. ("Thanks for your
       very kind note of February 22 [1942]. . . ."), MS 112, box 3, folder
       44, Bullitt Papers.
168   "became her trademark": Barton (2010), 102.
168   she briefed him: Ibid., 103.
168   legally changed her name: Ibid., 108.
169   "Langner seems to be": Antheil to Bullitt, 30 June 1941, MS 112,
       box 3, folder 42, Bullitt Papers.

NINE: RED-HOT APPARATUS

170   "We are, at present": George Antheil et al., "Idea for a Radio-
       Controlled Torpedo," 23 Dec. 1940, document in possession of
       Anthony Loder, Los Angeles.
170   "two sister system[s]": document in possession of Anthony Loder,
       Los Angeles.
171   "(a) The ribbon wavelength": Ibid.
174   "It's my daily work": Antheil to Bullitt, 24 June 1942, MS 112,
       box 3, folder 44, William C. Bullitt Papers, Yale University
       Library.
174   "Hedy was once married": Antheil to Bullitt, 20 May 1941, MS
       112, box 3, folder 42, Bullitt Papers.
174   "novel torpedo": Ibid.
175   "It is of course": Markey and Antheil (1941), 12–13.
177   "Recent communications": Antheil to Bullitt, 30 June 1941, MS
       112, box 3, folder 42, Bullitt Papers.
177   illness ran into the layoff: Shearer (2010), 130–31.
178   "Hedy was here Sunday": Antheil to Bullitt, 19 July 1941, MS 112,
       box 3, folder 42, Bullitt Papers.
178   "At that time": Boski Antheil memoir, 93–94, box 17, folders 1–3,
       Antheil Collection.
179   "Hollywood is a funny": Ibid.
179   "Let's move away": Antheil (1945), 335.
179   "We moved to a tiny": Boski Antheil memoir, 94.
179   "We got the smallest": Antheil (1945), 336.
180   "It was from my dead": Ibid.
180   "I have just finished": Antheil to Bullitt, 19 July 1941.
181   "HEDY LAMARR INVENTOR": *New York Times*, 1 Oct. 1941.

181   "actually reached": Antheil to Bullitt, 13 July 1942, MS 112, box 3, folder 44, Bullitt Papers.

182   "The Ambassador said": U.S. Department of State (1943), 136.

183   "When that big bomb": Mullener (2002), 31.

184   "U.S. submariners began": Wildenberg and Polmar (2010), 102.

185   These and other problems: See Gannon (1996), Newpower (2006), and Lockwood (1951).

185   "After considering our torpedo": Antheil to Bullitt, 5 Feb. 1942 (misdated 1941), MS 112, box 3, folder 44, Bullitt Papers.

186   "Hedy and I spent": Antheil to Bullitt, 13 July 1942.

188   "unquestionably dealt": Kennan, introduction to Bullitt (1972), xii.

188   "I am sorry": Bullitt to Antheil, 25 Aug. 1942, box 28, folder 16, Antheil Collection.

189   "during the anxious days": Antheil to Bullitt, 23 May 1943, MS 112, box 3, folder 44, Bullitt Papers.

189   "rebirth": Quoted in Whitesitt (1983), 57.

189   news analyst: Ibid., 58.

190   "chip in and help": "Hedy Lamarr Sells $4,547,000 Bonds," *New York Times*, 2 Sept. 1942.

191   "NEWARK, N.J., Sept. 4": "Hedy Lamarr a Hit in Newark," *New York Times*, 5 Sept. 1942.

TEN: O PIONEERS!

194   denied its identifying information: "It is only this year (1997) that the connection has been pointed out by Dave Hughes." Ścibor-Marchocki (2003), "Sonobuoy."

194   "When we received": Ibid.

195   "As requested": Ibid.

196   "In retrospect": Ibid.

196   "worked very well": Ibid.

197   "solves each": Ibid.

197   "spread spectrum": Scholtz (1982), 832.

197   paper published in 1982: Ibid.

197   told me he was aware: Robert Scholtz, personal communication, 28 April 2011.

198   follow-up paper: Price (1983).
198   "Although the radio link": Scholtz (1982), 829.
199   seminal paper: Shannon (1948).
199   "Shannon's formula": Walters (2005), 165.
199   coined the term "bit": Shannon (1948), 379.
200   "evidently carried": Scholtz (1982), 833.
200   different secret communication systems: Ibid., 845–47.
201   "scores of patents": Ibid., 835.
201   "For the first time": Ścibor-Marchocki (2003), "Surveillance Drone."
202   top four most performed: Whitesitt (1983), 62.
202   "It is a wonderful": Quoted in ibid.
203   "There is everything": Quoted in ibid.
203   "became a shuttle trip": Lamarr (1966), 129.
203   Traumas emerged: Ibid., 128–30.
204   "time and analysis" . . . "the crisp, competitive": Ibid., 131.
204   "It was the case": Ibid., 137.
204   "My judgment on scripts": Ibid., 166.
205   "We argued quite a bit": Quoted in ibid., 181.
205    $30 million or more from acting: Ibid., 312.
206   *Spread Spectrum Systems*: Dixon (1984).
206   "first comprehensive": Mike Marcus, "Early Civil Spread Spectrum History," http://www.marcus-spectrum.com/SSHistory.htm, 1.
206   "anachronistic technical regulations": Marcus (2009), 19.
206   "In the 1970s": Ibid., 20–21.
207   study the FCC commissioned: Scales (1980).
207   "Spread spectrum techniques": Ibid., 1–3.
208   "It became clear": Marcus (2009), 24.
208   "the spread spectrum Pandora's box": Ibid.
209   not so easily persuaded: This discussion follows ibid., 26.
209   "Legend has it": Ibid., 25.
209   "The rules adopted": Ibid., 33.
210   A study done for Microsoft: Perspective Associates (UK) (2009), *Economic Value of Unlicensed Spectrum.* http://www.marcus-spectrum.com/SSHistory.htm.
210   "I can't understand": Meeks (1990), 2, 4.
211   "Few people were ever": Osborne (2000).

212   "I wasn't worried": Dave Hughes interview with author, Colorado Springs, 23 Sept. 2010. All Dave Hughes quotations from this source.

AFTERWORD

216   "Some time ago": Boski Antheil, "Past Present," box 17, folders 1–3, Antheil Collection, Library of Congress.
217   "To neutralize Mandl": Newton (1986), 544.
218   "Hedy's fondness": Barton (2010), 227.
218   "living a very private": Carter (2009), 116.

References

Abelson, Hal, Ken Ledeen, and Harry Lewis. 2008. *Blown to Bits: Your Life, Liberty, and Happiness After the Digital Explosion.* Upper Saddle River, N.J.: Addison-Wesley.

Adrian. 1938. "Clothes." In *Behind the Screen: How Films Are Made,* edited by Stephen Watts. London: Arthur Barker.

Antheil, George. 1916. "The Madman's Narrative." www.antheil.org.

———. 1924. "Manifest der Musico-Mechanico." *De Stijl* 6:99–102.

———. 1925a. "My Ballet Mécanique." *De Stijl* 6:141–44.

———. 1925b. "My Ballet Mécanique: What It Means." *Der Querschnitt,* Sept.

———. 1935. "Composers in Movieland." *Modern Music* 12 (2): 62–68.

———. 1936a. "Glands on a Hobby Horse." *Esquire,* April, 47, 174, 176, 178.

———. 1936b. "Glandbook for the Questing Male." *Esquire,* May, 40–41, 184.

———. 1936c. "Know Thyself." *Esquire,* July, 34, 192–95.

———. 1936d. "So Smells Defeat." *Esquire,* Nov., 52–53, 227–28.

———. 1937a. *Every Man His Own Detective: A Study of Glandular Criminology.* New York: Stackpole Sons.

———. 1937b. "Hollywood and the New Music." *Cinema Arts,* July, 28–29.

————. 1938. "George Gershwin." In *George Gershwin*, edited by Merle Armitage. New York: Longmans, Green.

[————]. 1940. *The Shape of the War to Come*. New York: Longmans, Green.

————. 1945. *Bad Boy of Music*. Garden City, N.Y.: Doubleday, Doran.

————. 2000. *Antheil Plays Antheil: The SPA Recordings & Private Audio Documents, 1942–1958*. San Francisco: Other Minds. Two compact discs.

Baker, Sarah. 2009. *Lucky Stars: Janet Gaynor and Charles Farrell*. Albany, Ga.: BearManor Media.

Barton, Ruth. 2010. *Hedy Lamarr: The Most Beautiful Woman in Film*. Lexington: University Press of Kentucky.

Beach, Sylvia. 1991. *Shakespeare and Company*. New ed. Lincoln: University of Nebraska Press.

Berle, Alf K., and L. Sprague De Camp. 1937. *Inventions and Their Management*. Scranton, Pa.: International Textbook Company.

Bollinger, Martin J. 2010. *Warriors and Wizards: The Development and Defeat of Radio-Controlled Glide Bombs of the Third Reich*. Annapolis, Md.: Naval Institute Press.

Boone, J. V., and R. R. Peterson. 2009. "Sigsaly—the Start of the Digital Revolution." National Security Agency Historical Document, posted 15 Jan. 2009.

Braun, Hans-Joachim. 1997. "Advanced Weaponry of the Stars." *American Heritage Invention & Technology* 12 (4).

Brodsky, Ira. 2008. *The History of Wireless: How Creative Minds Produced Technology for the Masses*. St. Louis: Telescope Books.

Brownell, Will, and Richard N. Billings. 1987. *So Close to Greatness: A Biography of William C. Bullitt*. New York: Macmillan.

Bullitt, Orville H., ed. 1972. *For the President, Personal and Secret: Correspondence Between Franklin D. Roosevelt and William C. Bullitt*. Boston: Houghton Mifflin.

Carter, Graydon, ed. 2009. *Vanity Fair's Proust Questionnaire: 101 Luminaries Ponder Love, Death, Happiness, and the Meaning of Life*. New York: Rodale.

Carter, Kenneth R. 2009. "Unlicensed to Kill: A Brief History of the Part 15 Rules." *INFO* 11 (5): 9–18.

Clark, John D. 1972. *Ignition! An Informal History of Liquid Rocket Propellants*. New Brunswick, N.J.: Rutgers University Press.

Copland, Aaron, and Vivian Perlis. 1984. *Copland: 1900 Through 1942*. New York: St. Martin's/Marek.

Coward, Noël. 1999. *Private Lives*. In *Three Plays: Blithe Spirit, Hay Fever, Private Lives*. New York: Vintage.

Delson, Susan B. 2006. *Dudley Murphy, Hollywood Wild Card*. Minneapolis: University of Minnesota Press.

Dixon, Robert C. 1984. *Spread Spectrum Systems*. 2nd ed. New York: John Wiley & Sons.

Donald, James. 2009. "Jazz Modernism and Film Art: Dudley Murphy and *Ballet mécanique*." *Modernism/Modernity* 16 (1): 25–49.

Dönitz, Karl. 1997. *Memoirs: Ten Years and Twenty Days*. New York: Da Capo.

Dubini, Donatello, Fosco Dubini, and Barbara Obermeier. 2005. *Hedy Lamarr: Secrets of a Hollywood Star*. Munich: Edition Filmmuseum.

Engelberg, Shlomo. 2003. "Spread Spectrum from Two Perspectives." CSCAMM Report 03–09. College Park: University of Maryland Center for Scientific Computation and Mathematical Modeling.

Fitch, Noel Riley. 1983. *Sylvia Beach and the Lost Generation: A History of Literary Paris in the Twenties and Thirties*. New York: W. W. Norton.

Flanner, Janet. 1972. *Paris Was Yesterday, 1925–1939*, edited by Irving Drutman. San Diego: Harcourt Brace Jovanovich.

Fluckey, Eugene B. 1992. *Thunder Below! The USS Barb Revolutionizes Submarine Warfare in World War II*. Urbana: University of Illinois Press.

Ford, Hugh. 1987. *Four Lives in Paris*. San Francisco: North Point Press.

Fraser, John. 2004. *Close Up: An Actor Telling Tales*. London: Oberon Books.

Friede, Donald. 1948. *The Mechanical Angel: His Adventures and Enterprises in the Glittering 1920's*. New York: Knopf.

Gaddis, William. 1951. "Stop Player. Joke No. 4." *Atlantic*, July, 92–93.

———. 2002. *The Rush for Second Place: Essays and Occasional Writings*, edited by Joseph Tabbi. New York: Penguin Books.

Gannon, Robert. 1996. *Hellions of the Deep: The Development of American Torpedoes in World War II*. University Park: Pennsylvania State University Press.

Garafola, Lynn. 2005. *Legacies of Twentieth-Century Dance*. Middletown, Conn.: Wesleyan University Press.

Gralla, Preston. 2006. *How Wireless Works*. 2nd ed. Indianapolis: Que.

Hall, Gladys. 1938. "The Life and Loves of Hedy Lamarr." *Modern Romances*, Dec., 20–25, 69, 72–78.

Hecht, Ben. 1964. *Letters from Bohemia*. Garden City: Doubleday.

Hemingway, Ernest. 1964. *A Moveable Feast*. New York: Charles Scribner's Sons.

Horak, Jan-Christopher. 2001. "High Class Whore: Hedy Lamarr's Star Image in Hollywood." *CineAction* 55 (March): 31–39.

Hughes, Dave. 1997. "Nomination for Award for Hedy Lamarr." www .driftline.org.

Hughes, Dave, et al. 2006. "The Role of Hedy Lamar [*sic*]—Her Patent and What Happened to It." *Cook Report on Internet Protocol*, May–June, 109–12.

Imbs, Bravig. 1936. *Confessions of Another Young Man*. New York: Henkle-Yewdale House.

Jeffries, Zay. 1960. "Charles Franklin Kettering, 1876–1958." In *Biographical Memoirs of the National Academy of Sciences of the United States of America*. Washington, D.C.: National Academy of Sciences.

Johnson, Eric A., and Anna Hermann. 2007. "The Last Flight from Tallinn." *Foreign Service Journal*, May, 46–51.

Johnson, G. E. W. 1934. "Mussolini Muscles In." *North American Review* 239 (2): 118–27.

Kennan, George. 1985. "Reflections: Flashbacks." *New Yorker*, 25 Feb., 52–69.

Kettering, Charles F. 1947. "Biographical Memoir of Thomas Midgley, Jr., 1889–1944." In *Biographical Memoirs of the National Academy of Sciences of the United States of America*. Vol. 24—Eleventh Memoir.

Lamarr, Hedy. 1966. *Ecstasy and Me: My Life as a Woman*. N.p.: Bartholomew House.

Langner, Lawrence. 1951. *The Magic Curtain*. New York: E. P. Dutton.

Lawder, Standish D. 1975. *The Cubist Cinema*. New York: New York University Press.

Lawson, Rex. 1986. "Stravinsky and the Pianola." In *Confronting Stravinsky: Man, Musician, and Modernist*, edited by Jann Pasler. Berkeley: University of California Press.

Lehrman, Paul D. 1999. "Blast From the Past." *Wired* 7.11 (Nov.).

Lessing, Lawrence. 1956. *Man of High Fidelity: Edwin Howard Armstrong: A Biography*. Philadelphia: J. B. Lippincott.

Livingston, Guy. 2001. "George Antheil's Childhood in Trenton." *Neue Zeitschrift für Musik*, Sept., reprinted www.paristransatlantic.com.

Lockwood, Charles A. 1951. *Sink 'Em All: Submarine Warfare in the Pacific*. New York: E. P. Dutton.

Loder, John. 1977. *Hollywood Hussar.* London: Howard Baker.

Malik, R. 2001. "Spread Spectrum—Secret Military Technology to 3G." IEEE History Center.

Marcus, Michael J. 2009. "Wi-Fi and Bluetooth: The Path from Carter and Reagan-Era Faith in Deregulation to Widespread Products Impacting the World." *INFO* 11 (5): 19–35.

Markey, H. K., and George Antheil. 1941. "Patent Petition: Secret Communication System." 5 June. Box 28, folder 16, Antheil Collection, Library of Congress.

————. 1942. Secret Communication System. U.S. Patent 2,292,387, 11 Aug.

McBride, William M. 1992. "The 'Greatest Patron of Science'?: The Navy-Academia Alliance and U.S. Naval Research, 1896–1923." *Journal of Military History* 56 (Jan.): 7–33.

McGilligan, Patrick. 1991. *Backstory 2: Interviews with Screenwriters of the 1940s and 1950s.* Berkeley: University of California Press.

Meeks, Fleming. 1990. "I Guess They Just Take and Forget About a Person." *Forbes,* 14 May, 136–38.

Merkle, Paul, and Jacqueline McConnell. 1994. "A Historically Significant Case of Labor-Management Problems: The Newport Torpedo Plant Before World War II." *Journal of Economics and Finance* 18 (3): 301–11.

Miessner, Benjamin Franklin. 1916. *Radiodynamics: The Wireless Control of Torpedoes and Other Mechanisms.* New York: D. Van Nostrand.

Miller, Henry. 1939. *The Cosmological Eye.* New York: New Directions.

Mock, Dave. 2005. *The Qualcomm Equation: How a Fledgling Telecom Company Forged a New Path to Big Profits and Market Dominance.* New York: American Management Association.

Monnier, Adrienne. 1976. *The Very Rich Hours of Adrienne Monnier,* translated by Richard McDougall. New York: Charles Scribner's Sons.

Moritz, William. 1995. "Americans in Paris: Man Ray and Dudley Murphy." In *Lovers of Cinema: The First American Film Avant-Garde, 1919–1945,* edited by Jan-Christopher Horak. Madison: University of Wisconsin Press.

Morton, Frederic. 1989. *Thunder at Twilight: Vienna 1913/1914.* Cambridge, Mass.: Da Capo.

Mötz, Josef. 2010. *Hirtenberger AG: The First 150 Years: Anniversary Publication 2010.* Hirtenberg, Austria: Hirtenberger AG.

Mullener, Elizabeth. 2002. *War Stories: Remembering World War II.* Baton Rouge: Louisiana State University Press.

Nagorski, Tom. 2006. *Miracles on the Water: The Heroic Survivors of a World War II U-Boat Attack*. New York: Hyperion.

National Inventors Council. 1943. *Journal of Applied Physics* 14:385–88.

———. N.d. [1947]. *Administrative History of the National Inventors Council*. Washington, D.C.: Department of Commerce.

Nebeker, Frederik. 2009. *Dawn of the Electronic Age: Electrical Technologies in the Shaping of the Modern World, 1914 to 1945*. Hoboken, N.J.: John Wiley & Sons.

Newpower, Anthony. 2006. *Iron Men and Tin Fish: The Race to Build a Better Torpedo During World War II*. Annapolis, Md.: Naval Institute Press.

Newton, Ronald C. 1986. "The Neutralization of Fritz Mandl: Notes on Wartime Journalism, the Arms Trade, and Anglo-American Rivalry in Argentina During World War II." *Hispanic American Historical Review* 66 (3): 541–79.

Oja, Carol L. 2000. *Making Music Modern: New York in the 1920s*. Oxford: Oxford University Press.

Osborne, Robert. 2000. "Rambling Reporter Remembering Hedy Lamarr: Funny, Fun-Loving, Fabulous/Unpredictable and Unapologetic, She Was an Original." *Hollywood Reporter*, 25 Jan.

Paley, Steven J. 2010. *The Art of Invention: The Creative Process of Discovery and Design*. Amherst, N.Y.: Prometheus Books.

Piccirillo, Albert C. 1997. "The Origins of the Anti-ship Guided Missile." Paper presented at the 1997 World Aviation Congress, 13–16 Oct., Anaheim, Calif.

Pinch, Trevor J., and Karin Bijsterveld. 2003. " 'Should One Applaud?' Breaches and Boundaries in the Reception of New Technology in Music." *Technology and Culture* 44 (3): 536–59.

Pollack, Howard. 1962. *Aaron Copland: The Life and Work of an Uncommon Man*. Urbana: University of Illinois Press.

Powdermaker, Hortense. 1950. *Hollywood, the Dream Factory: An Anthropologist Looks at the Movie-Makers*. Boston: Little, Brown.

Pressman, David. 2009. *Patent It Yourself: Your Step-by-Step Guide to Filing at the U.S. Patent Office*. 14th ed. Berkeley, Calif.: Nolo.

Price, Robert. 1983. "Further Notes and Anecdotes on Spread-Spectrum Origins." *IEEE Transactions on Communications* 31 (1): 85–97.

Pyrah, Robert. 2007. *The Burgtheater and Austrian Identity: Theatre and Cultural Politics in Vienna, 1918–38*. London: Modern Humanities Research Association and Maney Publishing.

Ramirez, Ron. 2006. *Philco Radio, 1928–1942: A Pictorial History of the World's Most Popular Radios*. 2nd ed. Atglen, Pa.: Schiffer.

Ray, Man. 1963. *Self Portrait*. Boston: Little, Brown.

Roehl, Harvey N. 1961. *The Player Piano Treasury: The Scrapbook History of the Mechanical Piano in America as Told in Story, Pictures, Trade Journal Articles, and Advertising*. 2nd ed. New York: Vestal.

Rothman, Tony. 2003. *Everything's Relative and Other Fables from Science and Technology*. Hoboken, N.J.: John Wiley & Sons.

Russolo, Luigi. 2005. *The Art of Noises*. Hillsdale, N.Y.: Pendragon.

Sayler, Oliver M., ed. 1924. *Max Reinhardt and His Theatre*. New York: Brentano's.

Scales, Walter C. 1980. *Potential Use of Spread Spectrum Techniques in Non-government Applications*. McLean, Va.: MITRE Corporation.

Schickel, Richard. 1962. *The Stars*. New York: Dial.

Ścibor-Marchocki, Romuald Ireneus. 2003. "A Tribute to Hedy Lamarr." www.rism.com.

Scott, Lloyd N. 1920. *Naval Consulting Board of the United States*. Washington, D.C.: Government Printing Office.

Sedgwick, Henry Dwight. 1939. *Vienna: The Biography of a Bygone City*. Indianapolis: Bobbs-Merrill.

Shannon, C. E. 1948. "A Mathematical Theory of Communication." *Bell System Technical Journal* 27 (July, Oct.): 379–423, 623–56.

Shearer, Stephen Michael. 2010. *Beautiful: The Life of Hedy Lamarr*. New York: St. Martin's.

Simon, Marvin K., Jim K. Omura, Robert A. Scholtz, et al. 1994. *Spread Spectrum Communications Handbook*. Rev. ed. New York: McGraw-Hill.

Sloane, N. J. A., and Aaron D. Wyner, eds. 1993. *Claude Elwood Shannon: Collected Papers*. New York: Institute of Electrical and Electronics Engineers.

Slonimsky, Nicolas. 1937. *Music Since 1900*. New York: W. W. Norton.

Slusky, Ronald D. 2007. *Invention Analysis and Claiming: A Patent Lawyer's Guide*. Chicago: ABA.

Spiotta, Dana. 2009. "The Glamour Geek." *Vogue*, Nov., 110–12.

Stokes, P. R. 1998. "Hydrogen Peroxide for Power and Propulsion." London: Science Museum.

Stravinsky, Igor. 1936. *Igor Stravinsky: An Autobiography*. New York: W. W. Norton.

Tims, Hilton. 2003. *Erich Maria Remarque: The Last Romantic*. New York: Carroll & Graf.

Tuska, C. D. 1956. *Patents and How to Get One for an Invention*. New York: Dover.

U.S. Department of Commerce. 2008. *Patents and How to Get One: A Practical Handbook*. Lexington, Ky.: BN.

U.S. Department of State. 1943. *Peace and War: United States Foreign Policy, 1931–1941*. Washington, D.C.: U.S. Government Printing Office.

U.S. Navy Bureau of Ordnance. 1945. *Torpedoes, Mark 14 and 23 Types*. Ordnance Pamphlet 635 (First Revision). Washington, D.C.: Bureau of Ordnance.

Vaux, Patrick. 1914. *Sea-Salt and Cordite*. London: Hodder and Stoughton.

Viterbi, Andrew J. 2002. "Spread Spectrum Communications: Myths and Realities." *IEEE Communications Magazine*, 50th Anniversary Commemorative Issue/May, 34–41.

———. 2010. *The Foundations of the Digital Wireless World: Selected Works of A. J. Viterbi*. Singapore: World Scientific.

Waissenberger, Robert, ed. 1984. *Vienna, 1890–1920*. New York: Tabard.

Walsh, Keri, ed. 2010. *The Letters of Sylvia Beach*. New York: Columbia University Press.

Walter, Hellmuth. 1947. *Report on Rocket Power Plants Based on T-Substance*. National Advisory Committee for Aeronautics Technical Memorandum 1170. Washington, D.C.: NACA, July. Translation of *Bericht über die R-Triebwerke auf Grundlage des T-Stoffes, R-Antriebe, Schriften der Deutschen Akademie der Luftfahrtforschung* 1071, no. 82 (1943).

———. 1954. "Experience with the Application of Hydrogen Peroxide for Production of Power." *Jet Propulsion* 24 (3): 166–71.

Walters, Rob. 2005. *Spread Spectrum: Hedy Lamarr and the Mobile Phone*. www.booksurge.com.

Weller, George. 1939. "The Ecstatic Hedy Lamarr." *Ken*, 26 Jan., 69–71.

Welles, Benjamin. 1997. *Sumner Welles: FDR's Global Strategist: A Biography*. New York: St. Martin's.

Wernimont, E., M. Ventura, G. Garboden, and P. Mullens. 1999. "Past and Present Uses of Rocket Grade Hydrogen Peroxide." Paper presented at the Second International Hydrogen Peroxide Propulsion Conference, Purdue University, Nov.

Whitesitt, Linda. 1983. *The Life and Music of George Antheil, 1900–1959*. Ann Arbor, Mich.: UMI Research.

Wikipedia. 2010. S.v. "George Antheil."

Wildenberg, Thomas, and Norman Polmar. 2010. *Ship Killer: A History of the American Torpedo*. Annapolis, Md.: Naval Institute Press.

Williams, William Carlos. 1954. "George Antheil and the Cantilene Critics (1928)." In *Selected Essays of William Carlos Williams*. New York: New Directions.

Wong, S. W., and G. F. Gott. 1990. "Performance of Adaptive Frequency Hopping Modem on an HF Link." *IEEE Proceedings* 137 (1-6): 371–78.

Young, Christopher. 1978. *The Films of Hedy Lamarr*. Secaucus, N.J.: Citadel.

Zenneck, Jonathan. 1915. *Wireless Telegraphy*, translated by A. E. Seelig. New York: McGraw-Hill.

Zweig, Stefan. 1943. *The World of Yesterday: An Autobiography*. London: Cassell.

Illustration Credits

Frontispiece: MGM/Robert Coburn, 1938

Page 1 (TOP): © John Springer Collection/CORBIS

Page 1 (LEFT): Collection of An Pham, www.hedy-lamarr.org. Used with permission of Denise Loder-DeLuca

Page 1 (ABOVE): © 2010 Richard Rhodes

Page 2 (LEFT): Moviepix/John Kobal Foundation/Getty Images

Page 2 (BELOW): Courtesy of Filmarchiv Austria. Used with permission of Thomas Sessler Verlag

Page 2 (BOTTOM): © Time & Life Pictures/Getty Images

Page 3 (TOP): Courtesy of Hirtenberger AG, from the Hirtenberger AG Anniversary Publication, 2010

Page 3 (LEFT): Used with permission of Denise Loder-DeLuca

Page 3 (BOTTOM): © 2010 Richard Rhodes

Page 4 (TOP LEFT): Courtesy of the Estate of George Antheil

Page 4 (MIDDLE LEFT): © Bettmann/CORBIS

Page 4 (BOTTOM LEFT): Courtesy of the Estate of George Antheil

Page 4 (BELOW): Courtesy of the New York Public Library Performing Arts Research Collections, American Music Collection. Used with permission of the Estate of George Antheil

Page 5 (TOP): © CORBIS

Page 5 (ABOVE RIGHT): AP Photo

Page 5 (ABOVE LEFT): Courtesy of *Popular Mechanics* (popularmechanics .com). Originally published in the August 1938 issue

Page 6 (TOP): Courtesy of the Estate of George Antheil

Page 6 (ABOVE): Photo by Shlomo Sonnenfeld

Page 6 (LEFT): © Horace Bristol/CORBIS

Page 7 (LEFT): United States Patent Office, Patent #2292387

Page 7 (BELOW): AP Photo

Page 8 (TOP): Used with permission from *Stars and Stripes*, © 1945, 2011 *Stars and Stripes*

Page 8 (ABOVE): ESA/P. Carril

Page 8 (LEFT): mptvimages.com

Index